Quiet Retreat Teachings

Book IV: Ripples of Light

More by Geshe Michael Roach:

The Principal Teachings of Buddhism (author Je Tsongkapa, compiler Geshe Michael Roach)

Preparing for Tantra: The Mountain of Blessings (authors Je Tsongkapa, Geshe Michael Roach, Lobsang Tharchin)

The Diamond Cutter:
The Buddha on Managing Your Business and Your Life

The Garden: A Parable

How Yoga Works: Healing Yourself and Others with the Yoga Sutra

The Essential Yoga Sutra: Ancient Wisdom for Your Yoga

The Tibetan Book of Yoga:
Ancient Buddhist Teachings on the Philosophy and Practice of Yoga

The Eastern Path to Heaven:
A Guide to Happiness from the Teachings of Jesus in Tibet

Karmic Management:
What Goes Around Comes Around in Your Business and Your Life

Quiet Retreat Teachings
Ripples of Light

by Geshe Michael Roach

March 28 - 31, 2002
Diamond Mountain Retreat Center

St. David, Arizona

Diamond Mountain University Press
dmu-press.com

Copyright © 2011 Geshe Michael Roach

All rights reserved. Except as permitted under U.S. Copyright Act of 1976, No part of this publication may be reproduced, distributed, or transmitted in any form or by any means, or stored in a database or retrieval system, without the prior written permission of the publisher.

Ripples of Light
Quiet Retreat Teachings
Book 4

Published in the United States by Diamond Mountain University Press
Visit our website at www.dmu-press.com

ISBN-10: 0-9837478-4-9

PRINTED IN THE UNITED STATES OF AMERICA

Book Design and Cover by Katey Fetchenhier

2 0 1 1 0 7 0 0 0 1

TABLE OF CONTENTS

First Day: Thursday, March 28, 2002   *1*

Second Day: Good Friday, March 29, 2002   *46*

Third Day: Saturday, March 30, 2002   *79*

Fourth Day: Easter Sunday, March 31, 2002   *119*

Verses: Chapter Ten Master Shantideva's Guide to the
            Bodhisattava's Way of Life   *157*

Acknowledgements   *170*

Preface

By the power of this good deed
May any single living creature
In sickness or in pain,
Of body or of mind,
In any corner of this universe,
Be thrown into a sea of bliss.

And for as long as they may wander
In the circle of suffering life,
May they never lose this bliss.
May every one of them one day reach
The bliss beyond all other,
And stay there never-ending.

-Master Shantideva 700 CE

Between March 3, 2000 and June 6, 2003, Geshe Michael Roach and several of his senior students engaged in a three-year silent meditation retreat in the desert wilderness of southeastern Arizona. During that time he didn't see anyone apart from the six retreatants, didn't get any news from the outside world, and didn't even hear the sound of a human voice. However in order to fulfill a promise he had made to his students before he left, Geshe Michael came blindfolded to the edge of the retreat boundary twice a year to teach, and students came from all over the world to listen to these teachings.

This teaching was given in the spring of 2002, just about two years into the 3-year retreat. The retreatants had settled into the rhythm of the days and nights of practice, and the support staff was more comfortable, with a permanent kitchen complete with amenities like running water and propane refrigerators. Everyone was more relaxed, but still very conscious of our own shortcomings. We wanted our practice, our service, our retreats to be perfect. We were struggling against the limitations of the environment, our finances, and our own strength of body and will, and constantly missing the mark. Frankly, we all felt like failures.

In the middle of our despair, Geshe Michael emerged from retreat with this message of encouragement and praise, his new translation of the tenth chapter of Master Shantideva's *Guide to the Bodhisattvas' Way of Life*. This is the final and possibly the most joyful chapter, the one that covers the perfection of generosity. It is the one that teaches how to take our good deeds and use them to transform our world. It teaches how to perfect our kindness to others. And because it was Easter weekend, he used the story of Jesus' death and resurrection in a new way, to show how a situation that seems completely hopeless and full of failure can be turn into a source of miracles and transformation.

It is incredibly rare to receive teachings from a Teacher immersed in deep retreat, and our intention is to share the special wisdom and blessings of these unique teachings with you as freshly and powerfully as they came to us. For that reason, editing has been kept to a minimum, to preserve the expression of his solitude and realizations.

First Day:

Thursday, March 28, 2002

I'd like to meditate for a few minutes.

This is holy week, and that's the week that Jesus was killed. And I thought before each day's teaching we could talk a little bit about the story. I hope it's good for you. I very much like to think about it.

Jesus has been teaching for only just over two years in his home province, called Galilee. He has managed to train twelve very good disciples and the gospels say that he has another seventy disciples who are teaching and who go ahead of him to different towns and villages and teach. There are, I would guess, a few thousand people who really believe what he's doing. And there are many who don't believe. He has even been threatened by many people, including the established religious authorities.

Then there is a scene on the road. He is speaking to his disciple Peter, and he gives him a high compliment—he says, "You will be the one, the cornerstone on which I will build the church." Because the word for stone, *petra*, is like Peter's name. His real name is Simon—Shimon. Jesus has given him the name Peter and chosen him to lead the disciples. Then Jesus shocks them. He says, "Now we will go to Jerusalem for the Passover holiday."

And Peter says, "That's the center of the religious authorities and the occupying Roman Empire troops. It's very dangerous. Something might happen."

Jesus says, "Something is supposed to happen—something very terrible." And Peter says, "Please don't say that; you'll scare the other disciples." Jesus basically tells him to go to hell; he calls him the devil. Five minutes after telling him he's Peter.

He says, "We have to go." And so they walk down near the valley of the Jordan River, south. If it were nowadays I think Galilee would be like Vermont. Jerusalem is like New York City. Jesus has been sort of a lukewarm hit in Galilee—Vermont—but now he wants to take on New York City.

And so they walk towards Jerusalem. It's the Passover festival coming up to celebrate the passing of the angel of death over the houses in Egypt. Every Jewish male is expected to try to make it to Jerusalem for the holidays. The Jewish people have been brutally treated during the last few decades. Even before that, there were many Jewish people who have been captured as slaves. With each conquering army: the Greeks, the Syrians, the Babylonians, the Turks, the Egyptians, they have been captured, taken back to those countries. And so there are Jewish people spread all over the Mediterranean seaside—communities and synagogues. Great synagogues that are still being discovered.

Syn is a Greek root and the Sanskrit equivalent from the ancient tongue is *sang*, and *ga* is the ancient root for both synagogue and *sangha*.

And so there will be thousands and thousands of Jewish men and their families trying to make the pilgrimage to Jerusalem for the Passover. Things are very tense. The old king Herod the Great has died. He has split his kingdom into four parts. He gave Judea, the central province, to one son who was very cruel, and the Jewish people revolted, and then Roman troops have been sent from Italy. There's a large fortress in the middle of Jerusalem filled with occupying soldiers, and the central province, Judea, has been given to the governorship of a man named Pontius Pilate, from Rome. He hates the Jewish people; he is known to be very cruel.

They have destroyed Jerusalem only about sixty years before—less—during Herod the Great's time. And then Herod the Great has rebuilt the center of the city. He is a puppet king; he was ruling with the Romans' help.

What's so special about Jerusalem then? It is the site of the temple mount, and on the high mount in the city is the temple. The first temple site was chosen by King David a thousand years before. He decided to build a huge temple there. He couldn't finish it—his son Solomon has finished it.

What is the temple for? It holds the tablets of Moses, the Ark of the Covenant. The Jewish people, as nomads before David, have been carrying these tablets around the desert, wandering on a wagon. David says, "It's not right, we have to build a proper place." And they start the temple of Solomon.

And you have to understand that the Jewish people believe that the tablets are a doorway to God himself. The tablets, wherever the tablets are, then the divine being is there in the same place. It's like a door to another dimension. So wherever the tablets are God is there also, and it's the only place where you can go and be in the presence of God.

What's on the tablets are ten commandments; they are the same as our ten virtues. And I think it's very beautiful that Lord Buddha said, "When I am gone from this world, you can treat those ten vows and the other vows of the Pratimoksha as me. When my body has left this world, you should understand that those ten rules of life written anywhere is me. That is me. I remain in the world as long as those rules of conduct towards others remain in the world. They are literally me."

And it's the same idea, so every Jewish person from all over the Mediterranean—from Egypt, from Italy, from Greece, from Turkey, from Syria—they hope to come to the temple and be in the presence, especially during Passover.

Five hundred years before Jesus, the Babylonians have attacked the temple of Solomon. Destroyed it. And destroyed the tablets. So the Jewish people built a second temple. And they left an empty room called the "Holy of Holies." It's an inner sanctum. Only the keeper of the tablets can enter this empty room,nd only once a year. Because the tablets used to be there and that's the closest thing we have left of God. That keeper of the tablets is a position that is a thousand years old. By the time of Jesus, it is called the chief priest, head priest. It goes all the way back to the wagon which was guarded by two priests.

And so for Jesus to go to Jerusalem is a statement. He is going to the seat of the Divine Being Himself. And he's going to the seat of the most incredible empire that ever existed up to that time. This is the seat of their military power in the East.

Herod the Great has gotten his kingdom first by going to Cleopatra of Egypt, and then to Marc Antony in Rome begging for military help. "If you help me capture Jerusalem and the temple, you can make it part of the Roman Empire."

The Romans agree. They come a few decades before Jesus' time; they lay siege to Jerusalem, which is difficult—it's on a mountain and surrounded by very strong walls—but in time they win. They are angry it took so long. They destroy the city, they destroy the second temple, partly, and they install Herod the Great. He offers to build a new and third temple bigger than the others.

The Jewish elders, called the *sanhedron,* are skeptical. He's not a real Jew; he's from another country, Itamea, to the South. But finally they agree. He builds a huge temple; it is the size of six modern football stadiums. There are single stones of a hundred tons still there. And the power around the temple is very great. Each Jewish family pays a very stiff tax to the religious authorities, and they are quite wealthy.

Herod the Great takes the opportunity to build a fortress next to the temple—they share a wall. It's called Antonia Fortress after Marc Antony, his sponsor. And there are huge numbers of very well trained and violent cruel Roman soldiers, centurions, living in the fortress right against the temple. And so the scene is set for great tension and violence. The Jewish people hate the Roman soldiers. The Jewish leaders, the *sanhedron*, are trying to cooperate with both sides so that there is not a massacre. And now Jesus walks into the middle.

First they go to a town to the east of Jerusalem. Jesus' mother has a friend—there is a man named Lazarus who has died. They ask Jesus, "Could you please come and pray?"

Jesus comes to the house. He says, "Show me the tomb."

They open a great stone in the floor; he walks downstairs. The man has been dead for four days, but the mind is still in the body. He speaks to the body, he speaks to the mind, the mind comes back, the man wakes up. People all around find out what he has done. Lazarus is happy *[laughs]*.

Word spreads to Jerusalem, not very far away. Thousands of Jewish people from around the whole Mediterranean are converging. Jesus says, "It's time to go."

The disciples say, "You'll probably be killed."

Thomas, the one who they say doubted, says, "Let's all go get killed together with Jesus." So they walk to Jerusalem.

There's no room in the city for the pilgrims from other lands; they camp on the mountainsides around Jerusalem. The Galileans have a large camp traditionally on a hillside across from the city wall. It's a Sunday, last Sunday. Jesus says, "Go get me a mule. Tell the people I will be entering the city gate at such-and-such a time."

People nowadays think that Jesus was being humble. There's an Old Testament prophecy that the new king will enter the city of Jerusalem riding a mule. The religious authorities are very aware of the old stories. If Jesus wanted to upset them and alert them, the worst thing he could do would be to ride a mule into Jerusalem, and he does. People have heard about Lazarus, there are rumors of all his miracles in Galilee. People are ecstatic; they think that maybe the Messiah has come. Many think he will liberate them from the Romans. And they greet him wildly—people throw their shirts and clothes on the ground before the mule, people spread palm leaves on the ground. And so we call it Palm Sunday, last Sunday.

It's much too dangerous for Jesus and the disciples to stay in the city; they stay on the hillside outside with the Galileans. There are at least several hundred, many who have followed him from Galilee. There are the disciples, there are about seventy other close disciples who are teachers and organizers., and there's a large group of women who have been following Jesus through Galilee—wives of the disciples, other women who believe. Jesus goes to the great temple. You can't imagine this temple. Every day he walks through Jerusalem, goes through their gate. He goes to the temple.

There is a beautiful custom in the ancient Jewish synagogues—*sanghas*—that anyone could get up and give a talk if they felt they had something good to say. And so Jesus is allowed to stand in the courtyards. Especially on top of the temple roof there's a huge courtyard. And he teaches. And he's not shy; he criticizes the religious authorities very much. He's sitting in their turf. He's taking a great risk to say anything.

He sees money changers. You can't make your offerings, your yearly tribute, to the temple treasury in your own currency—you have to use silver shekels. So people change your money. They take five dollars of your Egyptian money and give you one dollar of shekels. Jesus is infuriated. He says you are commercializing the temple; he actually takes a whip and beats some of the money changers. If he wanted to cause trouble in the temple he's doing a great job.

The religious authorities on the day that they heard about Lazarus have already decided to try to plan and arrange for Jesus to be killed. He's teaching how to overcome the lord of death. They could use that knowledge for their own families, for the people they love. They could use it for themselves. They would rather be envious and jealous and kill him. So he has to move secretly to and from the temple, carefully each day.

On Wednesday night he goes to the home of a Jew who is collaborating with the Romans. Everyone hates this man. He wants to know what Jesus is teaching; he wants to change. The disciples gather. A woman comes in; she is known to be a whore in Jerusalem. She's carrying a white alabaster box—inside there are priceless oils worth a year's pay for anyone. She goes to Jesus and massages them into his hair.

The disciples are shocked. "You could have used this money for the poor."

Jesus says, "You don't understand what's going on. This woman knows that I am to die. She is giving me the traditional ointment that is put on a corpse."

One disciple doesn't believe; he has serious loss of faith. His name is Judas Iscariot. He goes the same day to the religious authorities of the temple, the chief priest. He offers to tell them when and how they can capture Jesus quietly. He does so for thirty shekels. Thirty shekels is the traditional price of a slave; by the time of Jesus it can only buy you a shirt.

The next day the disciples meet. Jesus asks them to come to a special place for dinner: that's tonight, Thursday night.

Every home in Jerusalem has a special small stone-like bathtub outside the front door. It has a little step in the middle of it and you pour water in there. And when a person comes to your house, they have their feet washed. No one washes the feet of a guest themselves; it's only the lowest servant in the house. The one who's been bought for thirty shekels. They come out and wash the visitor's feet. We have the same tradition in Buddhism; when you go, *"argham, padyam, pupe…"* it's the *padyam*.

Jesus greets the disciples. He washes their feet for them. He wants them to learn to serve people.

They have a final meal together. He breaks the bread, he gives them the wine, he tells them, "This is my body and my blood. Every time you eat, every time you drink anything, you believe you are taking my essence." It's not just in churches. He says, "Anytime you eat a meal, anytime you drink something then you believe I am in that and I'm inside you."

After dinner Jesus takes three disciples, Peter and two others. He tells all the disciples, "I am going to the garden of Gethsemane." This is a small olive grove outside the walls of the city. It's already pretty late at night. Jesus goes with the three disciples; he warns them to watch for trouble; he asks them to stay awake near the opening of the garden of Gethsemane. And he goes and he prays hard because he's frightened—he knows what's going to happen.

Then Judas goes and reports the place; he offers to take the armed thugs. These are not Roman soldiers, these are not even the men of people like Herod, these are local—like mafia—that have been hired by the chief priest and the other religious authorities. They don't have proper weapons—they have big sticks and a few swords, and they come to take Jesus.

They enter the garden quickly. Judas says, "The man I kiss in greeting is Jesus." They don't even know what he looks like.

Judas comes into the garden. He takes Christ in his arms, he says, "Master," he kisses him. And then the thugs come in, a lot of them: fifty, a hundred people. Peter draws his sword. The head priest's servant is at the head of the mob. Peter swings, he tries to kill the man. He takes his ear off. This is a terrible thing to a person working in the temple. You can't be a chief priest if you have any disfiguration of your body, especially your ears or face. It's worse than killing the man.

Then Jesus says, "Peter, what are you doing? Put your sword away! People who live by the sword will die by the sword, don't you know anything?" And he reaches out and heals the man's ear, and then he says, "Please don't mind Peter."

And so Jesus is talking about karma. If you do violence to others then violence will come to you. Only a fool would do violence, even to protect a teacher. You haven't learned anything. Because when you hurt someone and you see yourself hurt someone, then a seed is put in your mind. Always. That seed will come back and then you will see people being violent to you. The mob coming for Jesus is a result of violence in the past. Only a fool would do violence again.

And so we often talk, you and us together, we have often spoken about trying never to plant a seed like that in your mind. We talked about how to destroy those seeds in your mind that you put there when you didn't know that those who live by the sword will perish by it. We spoke a lot about how to clean those seeds from your mind. If you do it well you will go to what they called heaven, what we call paradise, it's the same place.

But there's another kind of mental seed maintenance that's very important. And that's what to do with your good mental seeds. We do lots of good karma. How to take care of those beautiful seeds in our minds? I think we often tend to concentrate on the bad seeds, and that's okay—we have to get rid of them and not create new ones by doing violence to people who are bad to us.

And so when I was thinking about what to teach—there are lots of small birds here, they are very lovely, they are good friends, now they come to us a lot—and one of them said, "You have to teach Master Shantideva."

I said, "Why?"

He said, "There's a director of a retreat center in Arizona and he wants to hear the last chapter" *[sounds of giggling and laughter in the audience]*, "the one you didn't have time to teach in New York."

So I said, "I can't refuse. He's taking care of all of us."

And I thought it would be good now to speak about the last chapter of the great *Guide to the Bodhisattva's Way of Life* written by Master Shantideva, because we have to know what to do with our good mental seeds. We have to avoid violence to others. We have to try to burn the old bad seeds in our minds, but I think from time to time we have to celebrate and we have to think about the good seeds we have. And there are special methods for making them bigger and bigger. Because we do a lot more bad karma than good karma, so we have to try to make our good seeds bigger. And it's a happy work, it's a joyful thing to do.

Then I'll say a little bit about who Master Shantideva was, because there may be some new people here—I don't know. He lived about thirteen centuries ago. He was a prince. Early in his life he met the Angel of Wisdom, Manjushri. He became very religious; he meditated a lot. When his father passed away, the king, the people asked him to become king. He didn't want to; he wanted to go and be a monk, but he felt responsible for the people.

On the day of the enthronement he came. He looked up on the throne; Manjushri was sitting there *[laughter]*. That's his teacher. You can't sit on your teacher's throne. Manjushri said, "You can't sit on your teacher's throne." *[More laughter.]*

So he said, "Well I guess I'll be a monk." *[Laughter.]* And he joined the great monastery of Nalanda, which is now in the area of west Bengal in India, near Bodhgaya. And you know the story, but I'll tell it one more time.

He was a great meditator, a great yogi, a great scholar, and a great good person. He developed himself highly in the monastery but he never showed anybody. He got the nickname of *Bu-su-ku*. *Bu-su-ku* means Mister Three-Thoughts. Only wants to do three things: eat, sleep, and go to the bathroom. He was an embarrassment to all the monks. They made a plan to expel him. They asked him to give a teaching in public, which the monks did on a rotation. It was designed to embarrass him, so he would fail and they would have an official reason to kick him out. And he got up on the throne, the teaching throne, and you know the story—he taught the *Guide to the Bodhisattva's Way of Life*.

The monks were stunned by its beauty, as we are. The ninth chapter deals with emptiness and wisdom especially. As he spoke it, he rose into the air. People tried to listen, some people could hear far distances—they had something like supermeditation. They heard most of the ninth chapter. He flew away. He was still talking a tenth chapter. Very few people heard it.

Later they found him in south India far far away. They begged him to come back,

"Ooh, we made a boo-boo."
He said, "I need to do other things, but here's the book I taught."

And the tenth chapter is, I think it must be the most beautiful chapter. It's on dedication. It's a whole chapter about how to make your good seeds grow in your mind. It's a whole chapter about giving away your good karma, because when you give it away, as soon as you do it, it gets bigger and bigger. It's how to give your good karma away.

I've asked Winston-hla to arrange people to read each verse as we go. It's a little long; I'm sorry if it goes on a little long. I think we will read the first verse and then I'll speak a little more, and then we'll take a break, and then we'll read the rest of today's verses. I think about fifteen people will come to the microphone and read a verse, and then we'll talk about it. So if Winston-hla is ready I'd like to ask him to read the first verse.

Winston McCullough:

(1) **Thus have I completed writing**
A Guide to the Bodhisattva's Way of Life.
And I pray that by this goodness
Every living being
May take up this way of life.

The way to make your good seeds bigger, the way to give away your good karma, is that there's a key. There are two steps. First, you have to think about the good thing that you did. And when you think about it, it gets bigger and bigger. There's no expiration date on good seeds. They can wear out as you get a result, but if you keep thinking about good things you did, they get bigger and bigger—in your mind stronger and stronger.

It's a very lovely practice to go home and just sit there fifteen minutes: tonight, think about the good things you're doing, the things you're doing well, the things you're doing right. Think about them. I think you don't think about them too much. And then we'll speak about how you give them away.

If you don't give away your good deeds, if you just sit and wait for the good karma to come back to you, it's a little foolish, because you just get one small result.

Maybe if you were kind to someone, then someone makes you a coffee later on. All the coffees ever made in the world came from kindness. And then when the coffee is finished, the good karma is gone. So we have to learn how to reinvest good karma. We have to learn how to make it bigger and bigger.

I always think of my boss, my holy lovely boss from the old diamond company days, fifteen years together. He was very wise. We started with nothing; we started with half a desk that we were using in another person's office. We shared half a desk and a telephone, and he borrowed fifty thousand dollars from a man, a Turkish man living in England, and there were many weeks when he couldn't pay me. But every time he made a little money, he wouldn't use the money, he would put it back into his business.

So in the beginning we had one small parcel of diamonds. That looks like a piece of toilet paper rolled up with some diamonds in it. But he kept using the money by putting it back in his business. He would never spend it on himself; he lived very modestly. And he didn't show off his money. Every time he made more money he and his beautiful wife Aya, they would put the money back into the business. They wouldn't be like pigs and just eat it and use it and then be without.

We have to be like that. The good karma we make, don't use it up—give it away. Reinvest it in the best place, the universal bank—other people. Give it away to other people.

Later on we bought a little safe; we hid it in the closet. One night someone broke into it, stole everything. Later we had a safe that was about four feet high, filled with diamonds. Later we had a small room, an armored room filled with diamonds and gold. He kept putting it back into the business. Later we had a very large room, with armor plating and fancy alarms and twenty-four hour guards and it was filled with gold and diamonds. Later we had two rooms like that.

But if you keep putting your good karma back, reinvesting in the universal business of helping other people—giving it to other people—it gets bigger and bigger.

In Sera monastery in the early years in India, the students all had to go and plant the corn. Fifty acres of corn, walking in the sun behind an ox and a man with a wooden plow. It was terrible work; it was extremely hard. And the monks were very careful; they didn't eat all the corn, they always set some aside. There's a special building called a *bang-dzu*, and you would keep a large building full of corn for the next year's crops. You have to replant it, and every year the fields got bigger and bigger. Because they didn't pig out on the corn. They didn't use it, they invested it.

So we have to do the same with our good karma. And then you have to decide where you're going to invest it. Who will you give it to?

So I thought first to talk about the good karma you do that I know about. I think it's a teacher's job to remind a student, very rarely, about how good they're doing. *[Laughter]*. I beat up these people all the time. It's not a joke; it's very hard for them. But every once in a while, it's a teacher's job to tell you all the great things you're doing. So each day I will take a different group and embarrass them.

I think the first group fittingly should be the people involved in the three-year retreat. I just want to remind you of your good karmic seeds. And then we will read from Master Shantideva and decide where to invest them—who to give them away to.

It's been two years now—this month is two years—and the retreatants have done… you have done very well. Very bravely and very well; I think it's because you did so much good karma before the retreat. I want to remind you what you did, because then you can dedicate, you can give away those seeds to others. Just remembering them makes them bigger; they crystallize in your mind—as a *vasana*, or *bakchak*—in the heart chakra; and they get bigger. And then you appreciate them, and remember them, and savor them, and then you give them away.

So I'd like to talk about the good karma you did before the retreat. I'll probably forget a lot of things—please don't mind—and I don't know what has happened exactly in the last two years, especially with other people. Nowadays the retreatants only see each other three times a year; during three months of the year.

One of you came to me. We talked together; we said, "Let's start a small school for other people."

You said you would be happy to help; you said you would give up a large portion of your income. And we got a small apartment in a very dangerous place in the Hell's Kitchen, and we started classes there. You paid a large part of all of the rent, also for the classroom. You were working in a major nasty diamond company. You used to come home every day exhausted. They worked you many hours of overtime. You were an executive there; you did the accounts for J.C. Penney, thirty million dollars a year. And you said, "I'll give it to the students. I'll help start the school."

And you moved out of your comfortable apartment, and you thrust yourself into public life, which is hard. It's very hard. You don't have any privacy after that, and you didn't have any privacy after that. But you took care of all the students—there were, I think seven or eight at the beginning. You came home exhausted. You made them soup on cold days; you made them iced tea on hot days. And the classes began.

And now thousands of people, I think if you include Mongolia, maybe hundreds of thousands of people have listened to those classes. And it was because of your hard work in the very beginning. We didn't have any help. It was very hard. And you did it and you didn't complain, and you helped everyone.

Later on, you opened a beautiful little bookstore in the Village. You struggled to pay the rent. I know you didn't have any money for food, I remember. You used to go and get a bag of French fries to have something for dinner. But you served other people for free. We started out with the idea to have a coffee shop but she couldn't bear to charge people; she started to give away everything.

It got bigger and bigger—it attracted people who needed somewhere to go. There's nowhere in New York where you can go sit quietly and read a book and have a free tea and talk to someone for six hours in a row. *[Laughter.]* Except the place that you started, the Three Jewels. Many many people came; I think you saved many lives actually. I think just your pet dog saved more people than many classes.

And you gave up your very fancy job and you became a nun, from the holiest lama in the world. And since then you have conducted yourself in a beautiful manner. Your face has changed; it looks like the sun. And with that karma you have entered retreat. You have to give away that karma now to other people. But you have to think about it often, what beautiful things you've done.

There's another retreatant who was a college student, I think nineteen or twenty. She heard a class; she came; she said, "Can I do something to help?"

You were going to the most expensive college in the United States on a full scholarship. And every day you took a train into New York. First you helped in the bookstore. Then later there was a crazy guy who said, "I think these tapes are great, we should give them to other people." You told John Stilwell, "Oh, I'll take care of that." And so you rented an apartment in New York, in addition to your college classes. You rented out all the other rooms; you slept in the living room on a couch; and you turned it into a factory for sending out tapes to people who wanted them, especially people in prisons.

Then you said, "How do you do all this stuff, how do you make these classes, these notebooks?"

We said, "It's all on a computer."

You said, "Show me how; I'll help."

You couldn't even turn on a computer. But within a year you were translating some of the classes from Tibetan and you were doing all of the notebooks.

Later on—you were a glutton for punishment—you said, "I'll take care of any travel problems." Many trips around the world to teach.

Later on, we were all trying to keep our vows nicely. You said, "I think it would be good to keep them in a book." We discovered this was the ancient custom, especially in the secret teachings, and so the custom of keeping a book came from your ideas.

You helped write *The Garden,* a small book which many people have—it has helped people, I think.

There's another retreatant, who also came to New York. You moved to New York—you didn't have any money; you didn't have any job. John Stilwell took care of you. You said you wanted to help. You took responsibility for helping to preserve the ancient books. You went to, mm, Bell Telephone I think, and worked with a beautiful woman there, a specialist, and the first book we ever scanned was done that way. You took responsibility. It is the single greatest book of the second turning of the wheel of the Buddha—it's the *Eight Thousand Verses on Wisdom.* You got the whole thing beautifully scanned; it took many months.

There are inside that book, very rare book, a thousand drawings, wood carvings, of all of the great lamas of our lineage. You went to a very difficult wealthy man—talked him into sponsoring the work—and hundreds of those drawings were put on the web, free. I saw a book yesterday from a yoga tradition which had many of those wood carvings there, and I was very happy because we made a point of giving them away for free. You did all of the work; the CDs free; and people all over the world use those thousand beautiful carvings of all our great lamas.

Later you volunteered to go to Russia and do the same thing with about a hundred books from our monastery which were burned and lost. They never made it out of Tibet. There was one copy in Russia. You went there, you didn't know the language; the Russians were very difficult at that time. It was very hard, and you did it beautifully and now we have all of those books back in our monastery. When you people here studied the *Heart Sutra*, when you studied the *Diamond Cutter Sutra*, it was those commentaries we used.

Later we found out there were precious books in Mongolia. You said, "I'll come and help." It was very hard; we didn't have any money. The libraries in Mongolia were asking for a huge sum of money to even look at the books. But you helped, we got the money, we paid them, then we went to the library and they told us to leave. I left; you stayed. You said, "I'll talk 'em into it." And you used your charm.

Within a single day you had all of them wrapped around your finger *[laughter]*. I remember they asked you to eat some of their most difficult foods *[laughter]*. And some very terrible things to drink, and for the Dharma *[laughter]*, you did it. You came back and lay on your bed for two days *[laughter]*. I remember. You were very ill, as was your assistant *[laughter]*. And now I have received illegal word that those books have been catalogued very nicely. The library is open, it's very successful—books that were burned, lost forever, are being found.

You did all of that work, you have to rejoice. And I think more than any other retreatant you inspired the rest of us. In many ways—some I don't want to embarrass you—but I think especially in the joy of sacred movement you taught us how to start, and in Mongolia and in India with the Tibetans we trained. You really inspired us to do those things. And there are many other things.

One retreatant came after those other three. She said, "I want to help too." At first she handled all the finances of... oh, at that time there were ten or twenty centers in India paying Tibetan refugees to save Tibetan books by typing them into a computer and then giving them away to everyone free.

You handled the finances, which is to say, you kept the centers going with no money. They would write desperate telegrams, letters, faxes: "We haven't paid anyone for months." She would write back, "It's coming soon," and kept it going, and helped find the sponsors.

At one point you came and said to the big American lama, "You're killing yourself, you don't sleep. You live off pizza and ice cream. You're not doing your meditations. You teach meditation to thousands of people—you don't make time yourself, properly. You go on retreat and get distracted by other things—you have to straighten out your own practice."

And she forced the issue, continues to force the issue *[laughter]*. And you did a great service to all of us, I think, and you inspired us, all, to practice seriously. You're deeply devoted to the highest practices; you're like a dog that won't let go, and you insist on that standard for others, especially me, and it's a great service to all of us. You have great karma to give away.

There's another retreatant who is doing retreat in a small island of retreat land near Santa Cruz. It's a special extension of our retreat; it has been from the beginning. You undertook a very special kind of practice—we spent a long time discussing, designing how to become a yogi in the middle of a family life. And you have worked very hard at it—you are an example for all of us. We feel your energy and your goodness. You had many classes at your home for people.

When the books on the CD-ROMs were sent out, you spent months and months designing a beautiful book. I think it was over five hundred pages long of instructions for people, free, and it was exquisite. People all over the world use it. People came up to me in places like Bodhgaya, the lamas I had never met—they said, "Tell the person who made that design it's so beautiful, it's so wonderful."

Later you took responsibility when we were teaching how to do purification of bad karma. You prepared special kits for people to do special fire ceremonies. You did all the work at night, in addition to a part-time job and more than a full-time job with your children. But above all, you have perfected the yogi's life within a family, and we are all inspired by you. Later you prepared thousands of pages of prayers for the retreatants. We still use them three, four times a day. We think of you often—you are an important link in this retreat. You constantly inspire us; you send us helpful things that we need.

There's another retreatant here. You went to one of the greatest lamas in this world, Lama Zopa Rinpoche and he was immediately impressed. He made you a director of, I think the greatest retreat center (so far, Winston and John) in the United States. Hundreds and hundreds of people have been introduced to great teachers there and great retreats, and you did a beautiful job to make it even better with beautiful cabins. You had great teachings there.

Lama Zopa was so pleased he made you the director of the International FPMT. This is, I believe thousands and thousands of students, in I believe over thirty or forty countries. It's a thankless job—these people don't get paid anything more than survival. It's twenty-four hours of e-mails. And you did a beautiful job; you pleased your lama so much.

Then we had an idea—I usually have the ideas and other people do the work and pay for them. We offered to Lama Zopa Rinpoche the *Diamond Cutter Sutra* printed onto silver plates with some gemstones embedded in them, to be put into the heart of the greatest Buddha statue in the world that he is making. And you said, "I'll take care of all of that." And recently I illegally saw the silver plates—they just come in the food basket you know *[laughter]*. Really, really. I didn't know what to do with them *[laughter]*. I sent them back. And I believe they are being offered to Rinpoche.

So you have done a very beautiful karma. All of you have so much good karma to give away right now. I know you have many teachers; you all have great wonderful teachers: holy Lama Khen Rinpoche, Lama Zopa Rinpoche, Geshe Thubten Rinchen Rinpoche, countless other great teachers. But if I have taught you anything, and if you sometimes think I am teaching you, then all of the retreatants, you should know you have pleased your teacher. I couldn't be happier. I think it's important for you to know it. I couldn't be happier or more proud of you, and during the retreat you have all—those who are here, those who are on extensions—you have conducted yourselves with great bravery. It has been very hard. Physically, it's quite hard. Emotionally, it's very hard. Spiritually, it is extremely difficult to fight with your mind twenty-four hours straight a day. And you have stuck it out;

you have done beautiful things. Everyone's expecting us to come out with smiling sunny faces—we got old. *[Laughter.]* People look tired: they have new wrinkles, more gray hairs. But you have done a beautiful retreat; you are an example to thousands of people that we've never met yet. And I thank you.

Mmm, the careladies, I'm going to pick on you now. *[Laughter.]* Before the retreat you did intense good karma. One of you, you were running a section of His Holiness the Dalai Lama's office in New York. You were arranging for His Holiness' plans to be fulfilled. You were working very hard. At the same time you were serving your lama. You were living on nothing. You were making beautiful books. You have made, I think an eight hundred page book of the ancient texts that we use in our retreat. You did astounding work. I sometimes take it out, I look at it, I can't believe it.

You gave up everything you owned. You had a house—you sold it. You dedicated that money to all of the retreatants, not one but to all of them. Then you said, "That's not enough, I'll be your slave for three years." And you've worked—I know how hard it is. We couldn't be here without you. And you continue to do more and more things. You have unbelievable good karmas; you can expect some shit to come. *[A little laughter.]* I'm not kidding. Okay? You're attracting great forces.

There's another care person, care deity. She was working taking care of children in a very large school system, a religious school system in New York. I remember you came to class one time. You were crying, because a child's parent had killed themselves. You had spent days trying to help them. You did that kind of work for years, without any pay. You worked hard; they didn't have enough help.

This powerful karmas you have. You both became nuns—there's a powerful, good karma—you have to give it away.

The third principal care person, you came quietly in your quiet way—you preferred to be anonymous. You did many good things. You went to the retreat center in Connecticut. You helped make that place ready for many many people. You became very ill from the work—you had tremendously painful treatments. You never told anyone; I found out. And you continue to serve us humbly, anonymously. You have incredible good karmas.

If you three were hoping to please your lama—one of your lamas—you couldn't have done better, you couldn't do anything better than what you are doing. It's extraordinary.

If people remember what the retreatants have done they must remember what the care people have done. I think it's probably more difficult than what we are doing.

And now I should pick on the director. You and Mrs. Director. You gave up everything. You had a fat job in one of the biggest companies in New York. You were teaching at Columbia University. We couldn't run the classes in New York—we couldn't afford the places where we gave the teachings—suddenly checks started to come. I never heard of this guy.

Later on you turned your house into a factory for tapes and notebooks; you sent out thousands of them. You produced thousands of them. I didn't even know much, I heard about it. You were working full time. Mrs. Director was having a child. You just did it; you both did it, you took responsibility, and you did it and you helped. Hundreds of people got free notebooks in New York. They didn't come from outer space. Someone was working over a full-time job and coming home, and he and his wife were producing them and paying for them, for much of the cost.

Then you gave up all of it, everything. You arranged for this land to do the retreat, you have taken responsibility—you have cared for us like our parents. Anything we need comes, it's like magic. It's embarrassing, sometimes before we ask it comes. So you can't waste those karmic seeds—you have to reinvest them. You have to sit down tonight and I hope you will do it for a few weeks and think about all the wonderful things you are doing, all of you. It's extraordinary.

There isn't anything going on like this. There are a few dedicated people who have done these kinds of retreats, but not many. I tell you honestly, when we went to Sera Mey monastery and we met with high lamas to ask advice, they looked at us with a strange look, "Three year retreat? No one has done that for, oh, a long time."

It's like going to a Christian church and saying, "I want to learn to walk on water, you know, I know you teach that." *[Laughter.]* They say, "Oh that was the old days." *[Laughter.]*

No, the reaction was the same, they stared at us and they said, "Three years? You sure?" And so you are reawakening an old custom. It's beautiful—I think we have done that in many things, but you have all set an example. I tell you honestly, not just for the westerners, but even the Tibetan Buddhists are very happy.

Likewise there are many people, I think many here, who gave a lot of their funds. They just freely gave them, as much as they could, and without that we couldn't stay here. We're not naïve; we know someone's paying for everything and we know it's expensive. And you have that karma. You have given it so freely, you haven't even cared if we know.

Other people came and built the places where we stay. You have that karma. Other people send us beautiful exquisite things that we need. We need ancient books: people… especially in Boston, people… especially one amazing American lama in Howell, New Jersey have been sending us all the things we need: books. One of the people here, I think is paying for many important ancient texts that we are using. You have these good karmas; you all have this amazing karma of these first two years. You have to think about it.

And the rest of you who have come here, we feel you. A few weeks before retreat, it becomes almost unbearable; we don't sleep at night because you are three hours ahead. *[Laughter.]* And we feel your prayers, we feel your wishes for us. We know that people sit at coffee shops and remember us, and we feel it and it helps us go on. It has been a great inspiration to us. We don't have psychic powers; we feel you thinking and praying for us. I think everyone here, in their mind at least, is hoping that we will do well, and we feel it. So if you have this karma; everyone here has the karma of the three-year retreat. You have to think about it; don't be shy, this is a holy practice, Lord Buddha told us to do this practice.

Think carefully tonight while you're driving home, while you're sitting in your tent or your hotel/motel room. Think about all the good things you've done to help this holy retreat. We are not great people but we are trying very hard and we are maybe some of the first to try this. It hasn't always been easy or successful in every way, but it is a statement in the universe.

This small group of people have decided that it's important to really try to reach enlightenment in this lifetime. So of all the people in this Earth, at least we are trying very hard. You are helping us—everyone has extraordinary good karma. You have to understand that. You have to think about it. And now you have to give it away to other people.

First, you have to clearly admit that you are doing some really goddamned heavy good karma and you have to pat yourself on the back. It's always a little mixed up with negative emotions and lesser motivations, but it's extraordinary karma, it's like an atom that's about to explode into a nuclear bomb. You are making that kind of karma as we speak. You have been making that kind of karma. You should—you *must*—think about it.

Even when you focus your mind on that karmic seed, it gets bigger. If you just remember what you did before retreat or while you are here, if you remember what you have done for this retreat, the thinking of it awakens that seed; it makes it stronger and stronger. Then it's ready to give away.

I'd like to take a break and then we'll talk about how to give it away, and who to give it to.

[Break]

So, I'd like to speak a little bit about how you do dedication, or giving away your karma—sending your good karma to other people, reinvesting it in the earth, in the place where it came from, other people, sweet holy other people. So let's say that you're one of the many people—I don't think we've met most of them—who come and help the caretakers. We often get a very odd meal like Japanese sushi or some exquisite Thai dish; we feel embarrassed. We're not like Milarepa at all. We have a sign in retreatant language: we go like that. It means somebody flew in today. *[Laughter.]* And not that the other meals aren't extraordinary. *[Laughter.]* You should know, I'm not exaggerating, we are served extraordinary beautiful meals constantly, all the time, every day. It's embarrassing in many ways.

But suppose you're one of those people who came to work anonymously, the best way. Then you have this good karma; now you have to plant it somewhere, you have to send it somewhere. That's like putting it in the bank. It's like reinvesting it. So for example, you could sit down tonight and think, "I washed dishes for Venerable Jigme Palmo for lunch. I dedicate that, I send it." And you could send it, for example, to one of your teachers.

We all have many beautiful teachers. Just in this retreat, during the break months many wonderful teachers are coming to help us. They fly from far away. They give up their work with many other people, they sacrifice all of their income for that time. They come to serve us, to help us, and each of the retreatants has been blessed by several wonderful teachers. So you could dedicate that good karma to that teacher's long life. "I dedicate the karma of this retreat to the long life of my holy teachers, especially those who are sitting here."

Does it help their long life? Can you make someone live a long life just by thinking it? For this you have to understand emptiness and how karma works. I'll speak a very tiny bit: it takes a long time to understand clearly, but when you meet one of your holy teachers, actually they are just a big lump of skin and arms and legs and a head, and whether you hear them teaching you or not all depends on your karma. Nothing is coming from their side, nothing. Everything you are seeing is because you served teachers in the past and you helped teach people in the past. That big lump of flesh is teaching you, you see it teaching you because karmic seeds are exploding in your consciousness.

And the karmic seeds are planted mostly by intention. If you truly intend to help other people, everyone around you all the time, then powerful seeds are being planted in your mind. If you learn this art of giving away your good karma to other holy people, holy sweet living creatures—all other people—if you learn this skill, then really you are just planting incredibly vast amounts of new good karma in your mind, and that will flower and you will meet that teacher again and again and again. And they will teach you until the day you reach Enlightenment.

So yes, this is extremely powerful; this is the way to bring the teachers to you. Think about the karma you did for the three-year retreat. Please think about some of it now. And then send it in your mind: say, "I send this good karmic energy to my teacher's heart, to ask him or her to live for a long life." And that is a perfect act of dedication; that's how you give it away.

Imagine that the power is coming out of your heart. Not your physical heart, but from the very subtle drop of consciousness that lies behind the heart close to the backbone. See it coming out as a kind of a crystal light. It's light but it doesn't have any color—it's like water. You can think of it as ripples of light.

You drop the good karma in a quiet pond and then the ripples start to go out, and they touch your teachers. They touch your teachers in the heart, in their heart. And that actually begins to work. And the teachers will keep coming to you; you will see your current teachers happy and well and healthy. And then you will see new teachers coming over and over, higher and higher.

So let's try now, just a minute, just a minute or two. Think of one of the good things you've done, for this retreat especially. And then send it to one of our sweet holy teachers. We are so blessed; we have so many. We have holy Lama Khen Rinpoche, whose kindness to us—you can't imagine it, and holy Lama Zopa Rinpoche, and of course His Holiness the Dalai Lama. And send this energy now, at this moment. Drop the good karma in the pond, watch the ripples go out and touch them in their heart, in the little tiny drop of consciousness in their heart. So let's do that for a minute or two.

[Silence, about one minute.] OK. Now we'll finally get to that text; I'm sorry to go so long. Master Shantideva's good karma is that he wrote the book about how to be a bodhisattva. And at the end of the book, he says, "I give away this good karma."

And then you need somewhere to give it to, and he gives it to all of us. And he says, "May everyone who ever lives learn to act like a bodhisattva, giving every moment of their entire life to help countless living creatures." Never stopping, never wavering from that one goal, your whole life, every moment of your life. And he sends it to us; we have been given that karma. Now I'd like to ask that the second reader read the second verse please.

Andrea McCullough:

(2) **By the power of this good deed too**
May any single living creature
In sickness or in pain,
Of body or of mind,
In any corner of this universe,
Be thrown into a sea of bliss.

When you give away your good karma, either send it as help for someone who's in trouble, or send it as something beautiful to someone who isn't in trouble. And these are the two kinds of love, they're called *maitri* and *karuna*: *jampa* and *nyingje* in Tibetan. And the first kind of love seeks to remove other people's problems. The second kind of love seeks to give them happiness. So when you send away your good karma, you can send it for either goal—to stop people's pain forever or to give them ultimate happiness. These are the two great purposes for which to send your karma, your good karma.

I'd like to ask the third verse to be read.

Ven. Elly van der Pas:
(3) **And for as long as they may wander**
 In the circle of suffering life,
 May they never lose this bliss.
 May every one of them one day reach
 The bliss beyond all other,
 And stay there never-ending.

I think there are three different basic types of people in the world. I don't know who's who and I don't presume to know. The first kind doesn't think about other people much; they are concerned about their own happiness. I think if you are not Buddhas already or bodhisattvas, you and I, we tend this way sometimes. Then there are other people who truly want to help people. And they do it in the immediate ways, they help other people who need money or food or places to stay, things like that.

Then there are special people who understand the true stakes of life, that it's not enough to give people food or money or place to stay, because they will still suffer. While they eat they are getting old. While they sleep in the place you prepared for them they are getting old. While they use the money you gave them they are getting old – the stakes are higher than that. We have to work to stop all pain, all suffering, even death itself. And especially death itself. And all forms of unhappiness forever.

So in this verse Master Shantideva's saying, "I send my good karma to help people in a short term way, but I also send my karma to help people in the ultimate way."

And then you meet people who say, "I'm helping people in the ultimate way; I don't need to help people with food or money or places to stay." But that's not how bodhisattvas live. Bodhisattvas are working constantly for universal plans—every creature in the universe—they are working for them directly. But if someone comes into your yurt and they look tired, then they sit down and you make them a cup of tea and you serve them. Bodhisattvas have to do both. I'd like someone to read the next verse.

Ven. Lobsang Chukyi:

(18)   And by this power may the blind
        Open their eyes and see the beauty;
        May the deaf hear the song of sound.
        May every woman with child give birth
        As Maya, the Buddha's angel mother,
        Did him—without a hint of pain.

This begins a whole section of the dedication chapter, where Master Shantideva is speaking on two or more levels all the time. There will always be two or more levels going on.

He prays first, he sends his good karma out to all blind people. And if you've known a blind person, it would be a wonderful thing to give them sight. And he sends his good karma out that way. Can it give sight to a blind person just to think about sending them your good karma? Where did the blind person come from? What made the blind person; why did you meet a blind person?

It's painful to watch a blind person. If it's painful for you, you must have done something negative in the past, so in a sense you have helped create this blind person for you, in your life. So if you pray sincerely for their sight, it will change. If you know the real method for giving away your karma, you can give people sight in this life. You can actually perform these miracles.

But on a deeper level, Master Shantideva is beginning a long section of praying that people wake up. He's sending his karma to people who are like sheep going to the slaughterhouse. We have beautiful cows here. They walk around, they like us now. *[Laughter.]* They stick their head in the fence; they get a cookie. Sometimes they look like they'll pull the fence down.

But every time you see a cow here it's kind of sad in our hearts because we know they are here to fatten them up and kill them. It's almost intolerable to feel it; we hear them crying at night sometimes for the ones who were taken already. They are innocent. I saw the way they were brought to the truck for slaughter. They were offered beautiful bunches of carrots, fresh carrots; they couldn't resist. They didn't know why the carrots were there; they were being led to a truck that would take them to the slaughterhouse. They are innocent; they are trusting.

And everyone in the world, all the humans, are the same. They are sincerely trying to live a good life, they are trying to help their families, they are trying to do a good job, they are trying to get by. They are merely trying to be happy, but they don't know how bad things are. They keep hoping for things that will never happen and then they are slaughtered. They are helpless as the cows.

And so the first prayer here is, "Please, wake up. Look at what's happening to you, look at where things are going, look where all the other cows have gone. Open your eyes." It's something very bad here going on, we have to try to stop it. It's not enough to do small good things, we have to try to stop death itself, suffering itself, we have to try to remove it from this whole planet and other worlds.

So the first prayer here is, "I send my good karma to all those innocent millions of people on this planet who are walking slowly to their death, not knowing, not thinking anything else could be."

Then he says, "May the deaf hear." Because often you meet people, you give them very convincing logical arguments why they don't have to die, why their body can actually change, but they can't hear it. They smile at you with a sort of smile that says, "A little wacky, this one," and then they're gone from your life. And they don't hear.

Jesus often accuses his disciples of having hard hearts. He says, "I'm telling you how to stop the pain of every living being, and you don't even hear it."

Then he makes a special prayer; he sends his good karma to every pregnant woman in the world. It's a very beautiful prayer. When I first read this chapter, which is—in the monastery we read this chapter separately, as a prayer oftentimes in the temple. All the monks will sing this prayer together, this whole chapter—I said how wonderful to think about the magic of a woman. She is about to give the most precious gift you can give, of life, at the risk of her own life. To be a mother is the perfect kind of bodhisattva deed, to know as you conceive this child that you are risking your life to give life to another is so beautiful, and for Master Shantideva to pray for them, to send his good karma to every pregnant woman—may they not suffer during the labor, may they give their child as Lord Buddha's mother did.

Lord Buddha's mother in Tibetan is called the *Gyuma Hladze*. In Sanskrit it's *Maya*. And when she gave birth to Lord Buddha he just popped out of her side, no pain. They say that holy beings are especially careful not to give pain to their mothers when they are born. And so we pray that every woman who has conceived a child and has that special suffering of carrying that child for so long and knowing the dangers of childbirth—we send our good karma to them, it's very powerful.

On a deeper level Master Shantideva is praying for the successful birth of every spiritual person. May you open your eyes and see the trouble we and everyone else are in; may you hear the instructions on how to stop it forever. May your birth as a bodhisattva be happy and painless. Next verse.

Amber Moore:
(19)   May those without sufficient clothing
Be suddenly clothed; may the hungry
Be instantly filled with food.
May those who suffer now from thirst
Drink fine fresh water
And other delicious beverages.

Master Shantideva begins to pray for people who will enter the spiritual life. You can't practice spiritual goals, the deep ones with meditation and very difficult study—how to understand emptiness, how to get to other realms—you can't do these things if you don't have clothes. You can't do these things if you are suffering physically.

When I first went as a young person to India, I stayed in a town in the Himalayas. It was very cold at night; there's no heating there. You just wrap up as well as you can. In the morning people would count the dead people, during the winter. How many people died in town last night from lack of clothing?

You can't expect a person like that to be studying or meditating, it takes basic physical needs. You can't expect hungry people to go to a dharma teaching and start studying and meditating and doing what they need to do to reach ultimate happiness. People who don't have clean water to drink. And so at the very basic level, Master Shantideva is sending his good karma to people that they should have the basic physical needs that everyone needs before they can start a spiritual path. Next verse please.

Sarah Brewer:

(20) **May every poor person there is**
Find all the money they need;
May those who grieve be comforted.
May those who've lost hope
Find hope anew, and security
That will never leave them.

If you don't have enough money to pay the rent, if you're always living in debt, if you don't know what you're going to do, if you have this kind of anxiety constantly, you can't practice dharma. So Master Shantideva sends his good karma to all the poor people.

Then he prays for people who have lost hope, who are grieving. Oftentimes people come to the dharma only after a major problem in their lives, maybe only after their husband or wife has died, or their mother or their child. And deep down inside they are very hurt. Deep down inside they have lost hope. We see many people like that come. They come to teachings when they've had this kind of suffering. And it's almost impossible to help them. While you are in a deep state of grief, while you are in a deep state of depression, while you are in a deep feeling that no one can help you, that there's no security. If people don't have a very basic mental security, physical security, it's very difficult to help them and teach them. So Master Shantideva is praying for those people. He's sending his good karma to them. Next verse please.

Kedron Brewer:

(21) **May every single being who's sick**
Within this entire universe
Be suddenly, totally, cured.

> **May every kind of disease**
> **Ever known to living kind**
> **Vanish now, forever.**

The main spiritual goals—seeing emptiness directly, meeting higher beings, developing ultimate compassion—they take strength, they take training, they take learning, they take meditation. You can't do that if you're sick. Sickness is one of the great obstacles to all spiritual practice. And so Master Shantideva's sending his good karma to people who are sick. Then he sort of reveals his real game. He says, "By the way, may all kinds of sicknesses in the world vanish from the world."

How is it possible that all sickness could vanish from this world? If sickness is something that you see in your world, painful, then it has come because we failed to take care of others in the past. If we truly dedicate our good karma to sick people, then slowly we will begin to see less and less. In your world there won't be any sickness, and you won't ever see a sick person, because there won't be any.

Master Shantideva is showing you the real point of his chapter: you yourself will be the one to remove sickness from this world.

I know that it's a difficult idea for many of us, and I think maybe you think I'm just being poetic or trying to be inspiring—it's not that. Each person here, sooner or later, will be the one to remove sickness in their world, from all other beings. We spoke about it before, I think it's worth mentioning again. How can there be—I don't know how many people are here—but how is there enough room for all of us to save the world, to be "The One"?

It's a question of emptiness. You are creating the world you see; the karmas in your mind are ripening in your own mind. You will become the one to save these people on this world. You will be the one. There are people sitting here who can see that. *[Pause.]* Next verse.

Brian Pearson:
> (22)   **May all those in any kind of fear**
> **Be suddenly freed from it.**
> **May those imprisoned be released.**
> **May those downtrodden come to power,**

> All of us living then as family,
> In harmony with each other.

You can't meditate on emptiness, you can't see emptiness, you can't do deep retreats, you can't serve other people in an ultimate way if you are in a country where you're not even allowed to do prayers. Master Shantideva's talking about political repression, especially of spiritual practitioners. It's not something that used to happen, it's happening now.

These things are still going on. And it's not just other governments, the American government did it to the holy native peoples who were trying to practice their own faiths. The Russian government did it to the peoples of Siberia. And they crushed the monasteries of eastern Russia—where do you think the books in St. Petersburg came from? They were stolen from monasteries when the monasteries were burned and the monks were killed. So all of the governments are doing it, our government is doing it. We are indirectly helping that; we are all like that. Master Shantideva's not a fool, he grew up in the court of a king; he knows politics.

He makes an interesting prayer in the second half of the verse. He says, "If the people who have been persecuted suddenly come to power, may they not start persecuting the ones who persecuted them before." Because it so often happens that when one group which has been persecuted assumes power, then they start to persecute the other groups in exactly the same way, because it's our nature, it's human nature; we all do that. So you can send your good karma to people in any part of the world who are not free to practice their religion as they wish to.

There's a very subtle repression even in this country. You and I have faced many situations where you can't speak openly about your beliefs in certain kinds of company or certain situations where you work, because you know you'll be labelled in a certain way. And so you can also send your good karma to try to change that kind of repression, very subtle repression. Next verse please.

Sid Johnson:
(23)　　May all of those who are on the road,
　　　　To anywhere at all, be safe
　　　　And comfortable, wherever they are now.
　　　　And may they without the slightest trouble

> **Find at the end of their journey the thing**
> **They left their home to find.**

If you think about it, everybody in the world at this very moment is either sitting at home, or they are someplace else that they've gone to, like their office where they work, maybe a grocery store. And then all the other people are traveling between their home and where they are going. I think even at the moment that we speak there are perhaps several billion people traveling somewhere, even if it's just across the street.

And so Master Shantideva sends his good karma to them. "All you people on your way home commuting through heavy traffic, you know, reach your home safely. I hope that you find what you went to work to find." And just pray for all the people who are traveling.

But there's a deeper level to this verse. If you have opened your eyes, if you can hear, if a bodhisattva has been given birth, if you have enough food, if your mind is basically stable, if you live in a country where you can practice, if you're not sick, then please accept my good karma. I am sending you this good karma, all of you people who are starting to try to find a spiritual way. Master Shantideva is sending his good karma to everyone who's just starting out, he says.

And you and I can imagine people like that, people we haven't met yet, people who will hear one of you teach someday. And you pray for them, send your good karma to your future students. All of you will become a teacher. Many of you are already teaching; it is a beautiful, wonderful thing. Send your good karma to your future students; they are just leaving home now. Next verse.

Alistair Holmes:
> **(24)   May all those who've left dry land**
> **To travel in boats or ships**
> **Accomplish all they set out to do.**
> **May they cross the dangers of the waters**
> **And then return safe to their homes,**
> **And the arms of friends and family.**

What a coincidence! *[Laughter.]*

You have to understand that getting into a ship in Master Shantideva's time was extremely dangerous, if you even just think about Columbus. You put, I don't know, six or eight weeks worth of food in your ship; you sail off to the horizon. After three weeks you know you can't turn back—you don't have enough food to get home again. You must go on, even though you don't know what's ahead. You maybe will die in the ocean.

We can read the stories of Lord Atisha's travel to meet his guru. He left from India around 950—or a little later—AD. It took him, I believe, a year to get to Indonesia. He went for one reason—to learn what you are learning today. And the stories of the dangers you get in a small wooden boat. You cast off, you try to navigate, you stop for food and water. People will just as soon kill you as give you food or water. And most people who undertook these journeys died.

So in one sense Master Shantideva is praying for them. But in a deeper sense, at a deeper level, he's praying for everybody who's had the courage to leave what they knew and go into unknown, uncharted waters. I think everyone here—especially the people involved in the three year retreat—you gave up everything. In a sense you cast off. You had no idea, maybe still have no idea, what's ahead. But you had the courage to leave. You had the courage to leave what was obviously death. And Master Shantideva is sending you his good karma. He says, "Everyone who's had the courage to leave security."

Everyone here—all of you—have left some kind of security. I know that it is very hard sometimes. I lived for many years in a small community in New Jersey; I believe most people thought I was a fool. I didn't have a regular job; I was trying to study with this unknown lama. And it was very hard socially, the pressure to know that everyone believes you are a fool. I went one day, something special happened; I met a man, he asked me, "What do you do for your living?"

I said, "I'm a cook. I cook at a church."

And something special happened and I knew he was thinking I was a complete fool. And I think everyone senses, we all do; it's hard for all of us to have left the normal life in the sense of people thinking we are intelligent or we have a good career or—it's difficult. And in a sense you have cast off from what you knew, believing that there may be something higher, and you are just sailing out to open water. You are very brave in a whole world you are swimming upstream in the

Mississippi river. You are very brave. Master Shantideva is sending you his karma to help you. Next verse.

Mercedes Bahleda:
**(25)   May those who travel a barren waste,
Or mistake their way, who wander lost,
Suddenly come upon new companions
And find their way easily, free of fatigue,
Without the slightest danger of things
Like thieves or wild beasts.**

Here Master Shantideva's praying—people who traveled in Tibet, people who traveled in India in the old days, it was very dangerous. There were no police, there were no hotels to stop at, there were no interstate highways, no airports; it was extremely dangerous to travel. And many people died. People just rode up on horses and took what you had and killed you. And no one even heard about it.

And so people would be very happy to find another traveler; it would double their protection. Groups would form caravans, travel together, and so on one level Master Shantideva is praying for people to find good companions. He's praying that they never lose their way. He's praying that they be safe from wild animals.

We live in a culture where all the really wild animals have been slaughtered. But in places like India, in the old days, it was just you and the tigers when you were walking through on a long trip, and there were many animals that would kill you. When the monks first came to Sera, there were herds of wild elephants who would come and crush the corn and eat it, and they just killed some of the monks when they tried to stop them. We live in a world where there are no such animals in our country. But it was a real danger in those times.

There's a deeper level here. If you hope to travel a spiritual path you need companions, you need friends. It's much easier and you are much more likely to succeed if you are living around other people who have the same vision, who have the same faith, who have the same devotion. One of the greatest joys of being in retreat here is that the people serving the retreat, the teachers who grace us with their presence, all the people who come to help, and the retreatants themselves are all very dedicated, they have powerful devotion. And it's a pleasure and a joy to be together with them, and it makes us all stronger.

It protects us from the fatigue of giving up, it protects us from the wild beasts which are our own mental afflictions. It protects us from the thieves. Thieves are nice, friendly, sophisticated, reasonable, normal people who come up to you and say, "Why would you waste a week out in that god-forsaken desert?" And that's for us the wild beasts and the thieves: they will steal your vision, they will steal your devotion. They won't beat you or put you in prison; they will say, "Let's go to a movie." And you will forget what you were supposed to practice. And so being with other like-minded people, dedicated people, is very powerful. Master Shantideva is sending his good karma that everyone should have friends like the ones we have here; we are so blessed. Next verse.

Matthew Gerson:

(26) **May holy angels come and protect**
All those who live in fear, with nowhere
To go, no path to follow:
Small children, the elderly, those with no one
To help them; those who cannot sleep,
Those who are troubled, and the insane.

Here Master Shantideva, on one level he's praying—it's a very beautiful prayer—he's trying to send his good karma to people who are lost, physically lost. And then to people who are mentally lost, they don't have a place to go. They don't have friends. You know people like that. When you are with them they seem OK. They share a cup of coffee with you at a restaurant. They go home and they are lonely for the other twenty-three hours.

They don't have any choice, they don't know about any other thing to do like we do. They don't have a path. And specifically, when Master Shantideva uses the word *gonpo* in Tibetan—*natha* in Sanskrit, a protector, a guide—he's talking about a lama, a teacher, a guru. He's talking about people who are trying to make the trip without a teacher. And it's hard for them. They will never reach where they are trying to go and they will be alone; no one will be there to protect them.

And he's sending his good karma, "May these people meet holy teachers," like holy Lama Khen Rinpoche, someone who will spend their whole life to help people for free, in the ultimate way, and put up with every kind of disappointment, pain, trouble, all kinds of hard times to help those students. May all living beings meet a protector like that.

Then Master Shantideva begins to speak about people in the world who have no one to protect them. He starts with small children. In the history of mankind, children have had a special place. They've never had any rights. They are considered possessions of their parents. Throughout history, even into modern times, there have been no legal or social means of protecting children. They don't have protection. The idea in our society that a young child has the protection of society as a whole is completely new, and it's very flimsy. People still believe a child is like an animal who is possessed by the parents and whatever the parents do to the child is a private matter, they don't have any other protectors.

The same is true of the elderly. When I first came to serve Holy Lama, there were many elderly Kalmuk Mongolians in our community, because they all came here after World War Two at the same age, so everyone reached seventy, eighty, at the same time. And so one of our main activities was to help them find nursing homes and then go and serve them in the nursing homes.

I had never really been in a nursing home. I was shocked, I couldn't believe it, it was like a hell realm. There's one in which people were just screaming all day and all night. There was another where you had to walk down an aisle to visit a friend and people were sitting on each side of the corridor and they would just reach out to touch a person. They would look at you with this look of utter misery. They hadn't even been able to even touch a person. The children come at the beginning once a week, then they begin to come once a month, then they come once a year and there's no one to help these people.

We would leave them, the Kalmuks, we would give them a rosary to do their prayers; we would leave a little Buddha image that they could have next to their bed. The next time we came back it was always gone. We said, "Where's the rosary? Where's the Buddha image?"

They said, "Is there any nursing home worker in this room?"

We said, "No."

They said, "Then I can speak. They take them; they steal them."

"Oh, why didn't you call us?"

"How can I call you? Those are the people I have to ask to use the phone. They watch us, they listen to what we do. If we complain, we don't get our medication at night, the bedpan isn't changed. They forget to visit us during meal time."

There's a blackmail going on in nursing homes. The staff is often underpaid; they are bitter. They oftentimes are abusing the patients and the patients can't say anything. They don't have a *natha,* they don't have a *gunpo,* they don't have a protector.

And then Master Shantideva goes on to talk about people who can't sleep. I think it's very beautiful that in a major philosophical work of ancient times someone would have the sensitivity to send his good karma to this simple disease that almost everyone has had. Almost everyone has times when they can't sleep; it's a great suffering. If it goes on too long, you move into a deeper level, depression. You begin to be depressed, you begin to feel anxious all the time, and if it gets deeper you simply go insane.

People who can't sleep are no fun to be around. People who are deeply depressed or have anxiety lose their friends. People who get into an asylum—if you think people won't visit old people, you should see the people in the asylums. We used to go to visit people. It's hopeless, it's very great suffering. People are literally beating each other, screaming, televisions are up full blast because no one can stand the sound of everyone else screaming.

And Master Shantideva's praying for those people; he's sending his power to those people. On a deeper level, people who are children—you know, many of you, it's a code word for people who haven't woken up yet—people who are still like children. They are walking very patiently, slowly, ignorantly, to their death. Everything they do to make themselves happy is backwards. Every action they take during the day is only giving them more pain. They don't understand; they are just like small children with a huge pack of razor blades cutting themselves. They don't even know, they don't understand.

So Master Shantideva's trying to send them good karma. Elderly doesn't mean old people. It means people who have lost hope. Half the people in the world are wrapped up in their lives. And half of them have finished so much life that they believe there's no hope anymore. People past a certain age refuse to believe there's any choice but to live the way they are living. It's particularly frustrating as a teacher to meet a good person, a sincere person, but who's gone past a certain age. You say, "You could learn to stop all these things, you could learn to change. You could change your body, you don't have to live like this, you could reach a holy paradise before you die." And they just don't believe it, they don't think it's possible. They've gone past a certain point of age where they can't hear it.

And so Master Shantideva's praying for them. When he speaks about people who can't sleep, people with mental anxiety, depression, insane, he's not talking on a literal level. On another level he's talking about people who haven't discovered kindness. People who are going crazy in this life because they are trying to serve themselves first, and this makes people crazy. If you are truly working for others, if you truly live for others, if your heart is stolen away by the idea of serving others, you will sleep like a baby. You will never feel depressed or anxiety. You can't, you won't; they all come from blindness. They all come from worrying about yourself first. All kinds of disorders of sleep, all kinds of mental anguish, insanity itself.

The one feature that characterizes all the insane people I've ever tried to help was that they were all wrapped up in themselves. They weren't thinking about others. Every kind of mental suffering comes from selfishness, from thinking about yourself. It's the great paradox of life, when you think of others your mind is at peace, you never have trouble sleeping, you never have anxieties or depression. So Master Shantideva's sending us his good karma to try to wake us up, because this verse is about protectors. And the only real protection is to think of others, to serve others. You will never again need anything, you will never again be hurt by anything. He's talking about the ultimate protection, which is simply living your whole life to help other people. Next verse.

Allison Cohen:

(27)   **May they spend every life they still have to live**
       Free of every obstacle to a spiritual life:
       May they find firm feelings of faith,
       And wisdom, and a perfect capacity
       For love; may their physical needs

Be filled, may they lead good lives.

He's saying if people wake up and try to practice a spiritual life, you know and I know the first thing that will come is obstacles. The more you try to live a good life, the more you try to serve others, you can be sure you will have obstacles. You become like a cosmic magnet. I'm not kidding, I'm not being poetic; it's absolutely true. You know it. People who have really tried to live a spiritual life, every time you step up the volume, the obstacles step up the volume. It must be like that, it will always be like that. You have to expect it, and you have to try to send your good karma to people who are already on the path and are getting obstacles.

We have this naïve notion that all the great saints of Tibet and India popped out perfect and didn't have any problems and served their lamas perfectly and kept all their vows perfectly and did the bodhisattva activities perfectly. Well then they wouldn't have been here, would they? *[A little laughter.]* You come to this realm, we come here because we are imperfect.

If you were involved with the Asian Classics Input Project, three or four thousand scriptures have been input—a good percentage are prayers to stop obstacles. Those books wouldn't exist if there hadn't been a hell of a lot of obstacles. So you can count on them, you can expect them. They help us.

Then Master Shantideva says, "All those people who are trying to lead a spiritual life, may they find first faith." The word *shraddha* in Sanskrit, *depa* in Tibetan, doesn't mean blind, stupid, unconsidered faith in a teacher or a religion. It's a word that reflects feelings of admiration. It's a word that means to aspire to something great and holy. And so the first step for everyone is to meet a person like His Holiness, the Dalai Lama, just to see him, just to hear him speak, or holy Lama Khen Rinpoche or Lama Zopa Rinpoche. You meet a great person, you meet a holy teacher. There are teachers like that I think listening today, and you are inspired by them, and that's what faith means. You say, "I want to be like His Holiness. I want to be like those other lamas. I want to learn to be as good and to serve people the way they do."

Then you need wisdom. Wisdom discriminates between wrong paths and right paths. Wisdom discriminates between something that's good and something that's not so useful. And all throughout your spiritual life—Lord Buddha especially emphasized it—you have to keep evaluating the path. At this point I need this, at this point I need this, at this point I shouldn't be doing that, and I don't think this particular path that I've heard about is very useful. And you reason it out in your mind.

Lord Buddha, as you know, taught four great systems. Three of them are wrong. But the lower three are necessary for people who don't have enough wisdom. And so a teacher will give part of a path or even a slightly mistaken path to a disciple whose mind is not ready for higher paths. Then it's really up to each disciple to find out the truth and to go higher.

All of you who studied at Sera with holy Lama Geshe Thubten Rinchen, you heard those teachings. In the third turning of the wheel on this planet, Lord Buddha said, "The fourth school I taught was wrong." He's already said the first three were wrong. Then he says the fourth one was wrong. And then he passes from this world. And so people are left with having to figure out which one is the right school.

And in the end Lord Buddha says, "You must learn. You must have wisdom. You must figure it out." You can't just take what teachers say literally. You have to use your wisdom. If you hear a teacher teach something, you have to check it out. If it doesn't make sense, you have to leave it. If you see something of higher benefit, you must drop the thing of lower benefit.

Then lastly you need love. We are all millions of years apart, possibly, in our spiritual lives. It's not just one life. There are people here who are maybe millions of lifetimes ahead of other people here. And so oftentimes it's hard to communicate. The person who's a million lifetimes ahead may be extremely close to the final goal. How can they speak to us? What can they say to us, how will we understand with the great gap between us? It's love. Love can break through all of those problems of communication. We don't always understand what people around us want, or what they are trying to do, or it's hard to make them happy. But if you have love for them it breaks down all the other differences. If you really love other people then all the other differences go away.

Then lastly in this verse Master Shantideva is praying that people who start a spiritual path should always have the things they need we need: basic housing, food, teachings. There are basic needs every spiritual person has to have. Next verse.

Ted Lemon:
(28)   May they have all they need to live, forever,
Without a moment's pause, as if they possessed
The treasure of the magic sky.
May they live together without ever quarreling,
Without ever hurting each other, enjoying instead
The freedom to live as they choose to.

There's a special thing called *namka dzu*. It's here, the treasure of the magic sky. It's a special yogic skill; it's a special skill of high meditators. They can like, reach into another dimension and pull out whatever they need. I need a cappuccino, right now. *[A little laughter.]* And they just put out their arm and they bring in a cappuccino. It's called the treasure of the magic sky. So Master Shantideva's saying, "I hope every person who tries to do deep meditation, deep retreats, deep practice, that they can learn this skill of the magic sky."

It's all based on generosity of course. These great meditators have perfected the art of giving to others. And so whenever they need something they can call on that karma and it comes immediately. And he's praying for that. What was the second part of that verse?

"May they live together without ever quarreling ..."

Oh yeah, OK *[laughs]*. Here Master Shantideva is talking about spiritual practitioners fighting with each other. If people are millions of years apart of their spiritual paths, it's natural that they would think that the other spiritual paths they see are wrong, and to struggle with those who follows those paths. I think it's important for each of us to understand that all of us are at different levels, we are at completely different levels. If there's such a thing as past lives and future lives, then it's very possible that people in this room are thousands of years away from each other. If person A stopped all spiritual progress today and person B worked for thousands of lifetimes, they might catch up. So naturally we see things differently. And naturally, different practices are useful for different people at different stages in their lives.

So it's especially foolish, and you are breaking your first bodhisattva vow, if you criticize other paths, demean other spiritual paths. Also I think it's important to say, especially in our countries, a person on a spiritual path such as the Tibetan Buddhist tradition just as one example, you have to be a real hardass, you have to be very stubborn. You have to work against the whole culture—the whole American culture is telling you from the time you are a child that it's important to make a lot of money, or that impressing other people is important. Or that it's important to eat a lot. Or that it's important to have good sex with many different people. It's important to indulge yourself. It's important to get what you want. There's only one life to live, live it as full as you can. Most of those spiritual ideas are just funny or they don't really work or they're for older people who have no other hope. And your whole culture is telling you that; the people here are struggling against the entire culture, hundreds of years of ignorance. It's very hard, people here have to be tough, people here are stubborn.

I think even if you could be with the retreatants for a few hours *[laughter]*...you can't stay in a little yurt for two years of struggle if you're not stubborn. And naturally, when we get together five or six incredibly stubborn people, we start to have little disagreements, speechless disagreements. *[Laughter.]* Within a few minutes. That's our nature. What I'm saying is if you go on a spiritual path, if you are working very hard, you won't succeed unless you are very stubborn. And then when you put stubborn people together, they start to have disagreements. Master Shantideva's saying, you know, "May all the people practicing spiritual paths live in some kind of harmony, even though they are all stubborn." *[Laughter.]* OK, next.

Andrea Spertus-Lemon

(29) **May every person who is small or shy,**
Who has no confidence, become
Strong and full of grace.
May those who've lived a life of need
And suffered from it physically
Recover in resplendent health.

Many of the early commentaries on this work—and there are many commentaries—they say Master Shantideva's praying for short people. *[Laughter.]* Master Shantideva's praying for people who don't have confidence. Master Shantideva's praying for people who have low self-esteem. Master Shantideva's praying for people whose appearance is not very beautiful—physical appearance.

But if you consider where the verse is located in the context, he is obviously not talking about that at all. There are two great lessons in this verse; the first is we have to be willing to take risks in our spiritual practice. We can't be complacent. You have to keep moving up. Every time you reach a new level, you have to go up to the next level. You don't get anywhere without taking risks. They should be intelligent risks; I'm not saying that people should just walk out in the desert with no food or water and sit down and meditate on a rock. But there comes a time in your practice—normally you're alone in your room, you're meditating, you have a chance to go up to another level. It's a little scary, maybe you're alone, maybe you sense that it might be a little bit frightening to go. But you have to jump, you have to take a risk, you can't be tentative.

And Master Shantideva's sending his good karma to us, "Be willing to take risks." You don't get anywhere if you just lay back and do what you used to do and what you're comfortable with. I think of any kind of physical exercise. You could think of weight lifting. People who are serious weight lifters always add another two-and-a-half pound weight at least every few days. They move up to the next level. They take a risk. People who are serious dancers, like ballet, they will tell you, "When I practice, I try to do something new. I try to push the envelope. And it hurts sometimes: sometimes I fall, sometimes I twist my ankle. But it's the constant willingness to push the envelope ahead that makes people great.

I've had the honor of having several teachers show me the yoga asanas, the physical postures which help your channels open. And several of them have had serious injuries in their practice because they pushed the envelope. And they are teachers now because they were willing to push the envelope, and they became great from pushing it, from taking new risks. Again I want to emphasize, it's not to take stupid risks, but to continue to push yourself. And Master Shantideva is sending his good karma.

I think the second half of the verse is talking about people who took a risk and failed. We, especially the people in retreat, we often try to push up to another level. And then we have a big fall. Maybe you spend a week in bed, maybe you think you're going crazy, maybe you get what we call a wind condition—for three nights you can't sleep; your hands are shaking. And so Master Shantideva is praying for people who took a risk, people who tried to push the envelope, and then they went a little beyond their ability. And he's saying, "May you recover." And I think it's a good thing to send your good karma, too. There are many people who have tried this or other spiritual paths in this country, and they reached a serious obstacle, and they seriously hurt themselves.

I have seen many students of many different traditions, physically, mentally, emotionally they pushed a little too hard. Perhaps they lost all their faith after that. Perhaps they actually hurt themselves physically. And Master Shantideva is saying, "Get back up, try to recover, and then get back to your practice. Next verse.

Gail Deutsch (Ven Gyelse):

(30) **May all who live in a place in society**
      Where they're not treated right transform
      Forever to a position ideal.
      May those who are looked down upon
      Be raised up high, and their arrogant friends
      Be tumbled to the ground.

Here Master Shantideva is talking specifically about people who in their own society are looked down upon. It could be because of their nationality, it could be because of their racial background, it could be because of their sex, it could be because of—in our country—whether they have money or not. But people who society, for some reason, has a prejudice towards. Master Shantideva, in his verse, is specifically speaking about women in ancient India, who were discouraged from practicing. Social pressures were put on them—you should have a baby, you should have a family, you shouldn't study philosophy, women don't do that.

I met women yogis in India when I was oh, twenty or something, and still it was difficult for them. A male yogi will get honor and a big meal, and then if a woman comes the next day, everyone thinks she's something dirty, everyone assumes she's kind of strange or crazy or immoral woman. And so Master Shantideva is specifically praying here that people who are in a place in society where they have strong pressures on them not to be spiritual should be able to overcome those pressures, and that it should switch. I think in this country there's a strong prejudice. People think that paths like Tibetan Buddhism are restricted to people who wear red robes or people who sit in a yurt all year. It's a kind of ignorance and a kind of prejudice.

Lord Buddha intended, strongly intended, that people should be able to live a normal life, with a family, if they choose to, with a career, if they choose to, and that by using those careers and families wisely, they reach enlightenment in this lifetime. He taught the secret teachings, the tantras, specifically to people who were engaged in business or in running governments or who had family lives. And so there's a kind of prejudice nowadays, if you don't wear a red suit, people probably won't come to hear you teach as much. If you lead a family life, people will assume that you're not having deep meditations and seeing emptiness, or that you possibly already entered a divine realm in your living room. And Master Shantideva is praying that that kind of ignorance and prejudice should be removed.

Then he does a very strange thing. Is this the last verse? I think it is. Then we will finish. I'm sorry it's so long, but I would really like to finish the whole chapter, and we have to do this much each day.

He says may people who are low in society get some kind of position, and then may people who are their arrogant friends tumble to the ground. What kind of bodhisattva would pray, what kind of bodhisattva would send his good karma to crush arrogant people to the ground? It's a special prayer. Master Shantideva grew up in the politics of the court. It was a very dangerous place, treacherous place. The royal courts of India were places of intrigue, assassination, imprisonment for the previous dynasty. He has seen the cruelty of the court. He was the highest, socially, in his whole country.

When he prays that those who are high should be tumbled to the ground, he's not praying that people should be unhappy. He's praying that people like him, who grew up in a high position, like you and I have grown up—we are consuming—I believe 10 percent of the people on earth consume 70 or 80 percent of its resources. We are in that 10 percent. We are in the higher edge of that. You and have grown up with tremendous comfort, rights. If the earth is being raped, it's because of the level of comfort that you and I are demanding and that we grew up with. And what he is really praying is that we should learn to fall down to the bottom, purposely. On purpose, you and I should be willing, we should see that simplicity is the real treasure. We should be willing to fall down.

You have to understand what it meant when Master Shantideva left the throne—you don't understand what a king is in India. A king owns everything and everybody. A king can come into your home without knocking, point to your wife, and say, "I want her, now." And she leaves. A king can walk into your house and take your children. A king can ask you to leave your house immediately, because he owns you, and he owns your house. This is what a real king was. But Master Shantideva gave it up to become a monk, a yogi. Monks dropped out of the caste system. Still in India, when you make that move, you become casteless. You drop down below the lowest caste. You are worse than an untouchable.

But Master Shantideva, Lord Buddha himself—Siddhartha, Lord Atisha, many great lamas of the past, they did this voluntarily to themselves. They went from king to filth voluntarily, because they saw it was best for them and for others. And so Master Shantideva is praying for all the friends back at the court, that they should be willing and happy to drop to nothing. It doesn't mean that we have to give up everything. It just means that we should be willing to live on almost nothing for practice. We should be willing to drop out of the lifestyle where career is the most important thing, and we should be willing to drop down to a much lower station, maybe a part-time job, maybe a pretty lousy car, maybe a pretty poor place to live, but simple and clean, and some place where we can do our meditations and reach high goals without all the distractions. So this is the meaning of this verse.

That's all I have today. I ask you, please when you go home, think about what you have done for the three-year retreat. Crystallize it in your mind. Don't think of it in your brain, see it in your heart, back behind your heart, a crystal drop. This is the main seat of your consciousness. In that crystal drop, your good karmas are ripening, flowering; and from that crystal drop at your heart, the world is appearing to you. So if you focus on some good things you've been doing, and you crystallize that karma in your mind, and then you send it out to one of the goals that Master Shantideva has mentioned today, which is mostly people starting out on the spiritual path. Send it out to them like clear light crystal. This is the level on which your drop of consciousness operates—it's not on a verbal level, it's not on a physical level, it's not on a mental level. The drop of consciousness deep inside you, which emanates the world that you are seeing, is ineffable. Power moves from one drop to another like crystal light, like ripples of crystal light. Try to imagine that level of energy, power, going out from the karmic seeds there. Then they become extremely powerful, and they can actually cause all the good things Master Shantideva has mentioned.

Please try it. We'll see you tomorrow.

Second Day:
Good Friday, March 29, 2002

So first I'd like to meditate for a few minutes.

Okay, we'll start. First I'd like to say I'm sorry we went so long yesterday, and I didn't know the time. And this morning I was thinking how to make it shorter. But I can't see cutting the story of Jesus, and I couldn't see shortening Master Shantideva's work. So we'll just take two breaks instead of one. So try to save some cookies and things.

Yesterday night, Thursday night, was the night that Jesus had gone to the garden of Gethsemane, which is really a grove of olive trees. It's a very foolish place to go for a man who's being hunted. If he had gone home to the Galilean camp, he would have been safe. There were hundreds of followers there. If he had stayed in a safe house in Jerusalem, there were too many supporters among the poor people for him to have been captured. But he goes to a different place. He goes outside the safety of the walls to a grove which can't be watched. His people can't protect him there, and he only has three. It almost seems as if he's trying to get caught.

Then they come, the thugs of the religious authorities, and they tie him up with his hands behind his back, and they lead him through the city in the dark. It's about midnight or later. Everyone's asleep. They take him first to the wealthy section of town, which is not far from the temple—it's on a higher level than the rest of town—and to a very beautiful mansion of a man named Annas. He's the former high priest of the temple. The position of high priest has been a very holy one, and very holy people have held it for a thousand years. In Herod the Great's time, just before Jesus, he imprisoned the former high priests. He killed many of the members of the Council of Elders, the *Sanhedrin*. And these high priests are sort of cooperating.

Annas is old. He has a sincere concern that Jesus will stir up the common people, who are very poor, and then the Romans will crush everyone. So he asks Jesus, "What have you been teaching?"

And Jesus says, "I've been teaching in the temple. Every day I come openly. You know what I've been teaching. I don't say anything secretly."

And then a guard hits him in the face and says, "Be more respectful."

Then the former high priest says, "Are there witnesses who can say what he's been telling people?"

And people come and say things, but they're all confused and contradictory and finally the old man is frustrated. He says, "Jesus, just answer me one thing. Do you claim to have direct contact with divine things, the Divine?" Because this is the special realm of the high priest, to be in contact with the Divine in the room, the inner sanctum of the temple, and only then once a year, where the tablets of Moses and the holy laws were kept, which is as good as God.

And Jesus says, "Yes, I do. I am in contact with divine things."

And the high priest tears his clothes from his chest and says, "A common man saying this is not proper. So I think you're guilty of what people accuse you of."

Then they take him next to the house of the high priest, the new high priest. This is the son-in-law of the former one. His name is Caiphas. And Caiphas is much younger and impetuous and less tolerant. And he questions Jesus and then, at the end, the thugs cover him, his head, with a cloth and then they beat him on the face. And they make fun of him. They say, "If you're a prophet you'll easily be able to tell which person's fist is which."

Then the *Sanhedrin* meets, or the few people left of the Council of Elders, and they make a decision that Jesus should be killed. But there's a question whether they have the authority under the Roman occupation to carry out any kind of sentence like that. So they decide to submit Jesus to the Roman government and request that they kill him.

This is now Friday morning, this is this morning, and the whole city is getting understand the truth of what I say. Other people listen to what I say and they get bored or tired or think I'm crazy. And they don't even see the other kingdom. I'm a king of a kingdom you can't even see perhaps."

And when he speaks about truth, those who hear the truth that he speaks, he's speaking about, in our terms, karma and emptiness.

Pontius Pilate says one more thing to Jesus. It's the last thing he will ever say to Jesus. He says, "What is truth?" It means, every person sees the truth a different way, don't they? "Thou sayest." Even if there was truth that you could tell people that they wouldn't have to die any more, how many people could hear it? Each person sees those words differently. Some people think it's just loose talk or silly talk. Some people, a few people, hear it, the truth of it, and then they act on it and they enter a different kingdom.

Pontius Pilate goes out to the porch. He approaches the religious leaders. He says, "I find no fault in this just man."

It's an extraordinary conversation they've had. I sometimes wonder who recorded it. It almost seems as if Pontius Pilate is part of the plan, some kind of bigger plan.

[Pause.]

So we've been talking about Master Shantideva's chapter on how to send your good karma to help other people. We first talk about how to send your good karma away, and then we try to talk about some kind of specific good karma, and I try to remind each of you of a good karma I know you have. And I know you have many that I don't know about. And then we go to Master Shantideva's text to get some hints about where to send our good karma, because he sees so much more than we do.

I'd like to repeat the method to give away your good karma. It's a seed in your mind. Most people aren't aware of the seeds in their own minds. When I say "seed in your mind," I think you think of an apple seed halfway between your ears. Try to think of it like a tiny sliver of diamond or crystal. And it's in a tiny dot, a crystal dot like water, that is at the level of your heart, behind your physical heart, near your backbone.

And imagine, or understand that actually, things are emanating from that drop. You are seeing the world you see as a reflection of that drop. Everything from the drop to the stars, and all the stars are being projected for you from that drop in your own heart. When you look up and see the moon you are seeing a part of your own consciousness. When you look up and see the sun you are seeing an expression of your own mind. And when you see other people they are expressions of your own mind.

So is mine the only mind in the world? No, not at all. They are real, the other people are real, and they are different from you. It's not contradictory to say they are different and your mind is creating them. They are different people created by your mind. And you don't have a choice. You know that. The last person who irritated you just before the teaching—it's your past seeds creating present results.

And so there are three levels at which we can change reality: there are three methods of going to heaven. The most primitive one is to try to manipulate outer events. I like to think of it like cement. I learned a lot about cement when we built Holy Lama, perfect *[cries]* Khen Rinpoche's sidewalk, and I didn't know about cement. We tried to make his sidewalk. I remember Venerable Chunyi-hla was there. She ripped her hands open, bleeding, to make it nice. But you learn that after it hardens, after a half hour or forty-five minutes, it's too late to do anything. You can scratch your name in it with a nail, but you can't change it much.

Outer events are like that. We can't do a lot to help other people in the outer world. We can try to feed people or give them money, a place to stay, but it's very limited. We run out of money quickly. You know that. You can only put so many people in your living room in New York. And there are so many more who need help. It's very limited. It's a good thing to do; all bodhisattvas do those things; we must do those things. But it's not very powerful.

Then there's an inner method. If the whole universe that you perceive is an expression of a tiny drop of consciousness, *bindu*, in your *tigle*, in your own heart, then it would be extremely powerful to go there and manipulate the seeds. This is what dedication is all about. This is what we are doing during this teaching. Go to the inner drop. Go to the chromosomes, to the DNA chains. Make subtle changes. And then for fifty, sixty, seventy years after that, the child changes, grows in a different way. It's very powerful.

I worked in the diamond business. I told you we had many other gemstones. One is topaz. I think I told you before. The blue color is made by radiation in a nuclear reactor. And I studied it because I wanted to be sure, that the women especially in our department were safe, especially the ones who were pregnant. It just takes a single stray particle from a single atom of a radioactive substance. It penetrates the skin easily, and it collides with a single small part of the DNA chain in a single cell of the mother, and then the baby will be deformed for his whole life.

Karma is just like that. If you really want to change reality, if you hope to bring other sweet, holy living creatures to paradise, it's very powerful to work at the level of the subtle drop of consciousness. And that's what we are doing when we make dedication. If your motivation is strong and sincere, if you truly crystallize in your mind your own good deeds, think about them, clarify in your mind the beauty of your own good deeds, make them into a beautiful little crystal packet, and then send it out.

Imagine it as a ray of colorless light, crystal light, coming from your heart, from that tiny drop, and it strikes the heart of the person you hope to help. Intention creates all things. And so you will be in a position to help every living creature, just with the power of your focus and your concentration and your pure intention. So I think it's a very holy practice. Just for a few minutes, maybe in the evening. I like to do it before going to bed. I search for one stray good thought from the whole day and I crystallize it by focusing on it and then I try to send it to another person's heart, to help them.

And there's a third method. We are sort of hardheaded. We have trouble believing what I just said about the drop of consciousness and seeds of karma. But I think most of you have advanced far enough to know that the external kinds of help are also limited. We are limited in what we can do, because that's like hard cement, and the inner drop is like wet cement. You can do anything with wet cement. You can make anything you like, because you are working at the cause level. You are working in the realm of causes and not in the realm of things that have already hardened. It's a very profound statement. We have to work in the realm of causes and not in the realm of results. The results are hard. You can't move them. The causes are fluid, like wet cement.

There's a middle ground, which is sort of a joyful place to be. It's a way to work down to the subtle drop. It's a kind of dedication that is more physical and easier to believe, and I would like to share it with you. I believe it very much. I enjoy it a lot. I think it's a very joyful and beautiful practice. And it's like this: You undertake a virtuous project, a good project. You design something to help other people. It could be building something for a lama like Khen Rinpoche, or it could be just making them dinner, for example. We used to do it in Howell a lot.

You go to the store, you spend a few hours. Those of you who are caretakers, I think among all the retreatants I can appreciate what you are doing. For eight years I went to the store, stood in those stupid lines, read the *National Enquirer*—from three feet away, because I'm a monk. So you do this, and then you go home.

And Rinpoche always liked to have a good *mo-mo*, a meat dumpling. It's a lot of work. It takes maybe an hour and a half. You chop the *chinse*, the celery, special celery; you grind the *erma*, which is a special Chinese pepper, in a mortar and pestle; you grease up the *mo-mo* pots; you chop the meat—he liked it chopped by hand. "No you can't use an electric machine on my meat. I like it chopped by hand."

So you make hamburger with a cleaver. And then you mix it up, and it takes about a half an hour to roll out the dough and press it into those nice little shapes. And then you cook it in the *mo-mo* pot and you hope they don't fall apart.

And then just about time you're ready to take it up and see the beautiful look on his face of happiness, a student walks in. They've been sitting in the next room reading a dharma book for the last two hours, not helping. And you make the arrangement on the tray, a beautiful arrangement, and you get a nice beautiful lacquered tray, and it's going to be taken up to Khen Rinpoche, and you say to this person, "Come here. You know, you take the tray up."

And of course they say, "Sure." And then they go up the stairs and you can feel Rinpoche's smile from downstairs while you're washing the pots. And you've just dedicated your good karma.

You see? It's a wonderful practice. I encourage you to try it. You have given away the good karma at the last minute. Think how this person feels. Rinpoche isn't supposed to know they didn't cook the *mo-mos*. He looks up. The tray is in their arms. He gives them this huge smile. His beautiful little dog is leaping up and down with joy *[laughs]*, because she ate more than he did. And this person, who maybe perhaps didn't have the strength to execute this little virtuous project, gets the credit. And they get this emotion at the end. They feel like they cooked the *mo-mos*, and they feel like they are offering it to Khen Rinpoche, and it plants a powerful seed in their mind for the future. And so you have given away your virtue at the last minute. It's a beautiful way to live.

We did it with his house. We built the two-story part. It was very hard. He left for India. He said, "Have it done before I get back."

It was winter. We didn't have much money. We had to do most of the work ourselves. And it was very discouraging that almost no one came to help, maybe a few people. Some people even came and watched us working. One person, I remember, came and demanded that we leave and take him to the store to buy groceries. But at the end, when the whole house was finished, there was only one thing left to do, and that was put the tiles on the floor. Even a small child can do this. You paint the floor with glue and you just slap the tile down. We invited all the people who didn't help. We enticed them with huge pizzas. And at the last minute we said, "Come and help us put the tiles down." It took them maybe half an hour. The building took a year. And we gave away the karma at the last minute. And for years people would come and point to the building and say, "I helped finish that."

And it's a good thing. You are giving away your virtue at the last minute. So I encourage you to think about this special practice. You do the hard work. You get things pretty much finished. And then at the last minute, give it away to other people. And then the virtue, the goodness, it spreads to their hearts in a way that you can see more clearly than in meditation. This is like half-finished cement, half dry. You are working in the realm of cause and result. But I think it's very concrete, it's something you can see and appreciate and take joy in. It also overcomes your habit, or the tendency we all have to try and own the virtuous things we do.

I'd like today to remind you about all your good karmas. Tonight when you try this crystal seed idea, you're going to have to pick a good karma. I think it's one of my jobs to remind you about all the good things you're doing. Yesterday we spoke about the good karma of a three-year retreat and how hard people work to support us—I think hundreds of people have contributed. The few of us here in retreat are so blessed to have so many people working for us. And it takes that many, I think.

I'd like to speak about the good karma that I've seen you do that relates to your personal practice, your own attempt to help all living creatures. The first and perhaps the greatest karma each of you has done was done before I met you. I know one person who has come to these teachings, here and elsewhere, who had four sons. She desperately wanted a daughter. Her fifth child was a daughter. She was so happy. Her husband and her daughter went on a trip. They stopped at a highway rest stop. A huge truck came and crushed them. The daughter died. The husband was crippled for a long time. That's why she came to the Dharma.

I have seen people coming to these teachings because their mother was killed by an ax by intruders to their home when they were a young child. I have seen people come to these teachings because they went home when they were five years old and saw daddy had hanged himself. I have seen people come to these teachings because they had AIDS and they were about to die, and they died. I have seen people come to these teachings because their sister as a teenager hitchhiked somewhere and disappeared and is presumed dead. I have seen people come here to the teachings because their mother lay down and opened her mouth and all the blood in her body came out, and she died. There are people here whose beloved brothers fell from a cliff and died. There are people here whose parents went mad when they were children, and they grew up with that. There are people here who were abused as children. There are people here who were raped by muggers. There are people here who were sent to a war, killed many people, saw many of their friends killed. There are people here whose parents left them. There are many, many people here who saw their parents hitting each other, fighting.

I could go on. I've spoken to many of you privately. I apologize if I've said something you didn't want people to hear, but I think it's important. The greatest good karma you have to give to other people is the very fact that you have come here. You have made a decision that life is suffering. You have made a strong decision to fight against that suffering. You made that decision before I met you. It's the greatest karma you ever did. You saw suffering, and you said, "That's not good. I will try and stop it."

You stay here even when it's hard. You stay here even when you have doubts. Because you believe maybe you can help stop suffering—your own and other people's. And I tell you honestly you learned that long before I met you, and you were strong enough to go and look for a way to stop the suffering. Any time you are feeling sad, any time you feel that you are not going very well, you remember the greatest karma you ever did. You had the strength and the courage, among all the people in this country, to say, "I don't want people to suffer like that. I'm going to try to stop it."

And I rejoice and I salute your strength and your bravery. This is something you did long ago. You can always give away that karma, every time you remember why you came to this path. That karma gets stronger and stronger every time you send it to another person's heart. That seed, that very beginning of your own personal practice gets bigger and bigger. Then you will actually be able to stop other people's pain. And I'll say the other good karmas I've seen, but I don't think they're as amazing as the first.

The main key of our practice is kindness to other people. I have watched you struggle to be kind to other people, as your teacher. I have watched you in groups. I have watched you coming home from work. I have watched you work with your families. I have seen you struggle to be kind. You thought no one was noticing. I saw you struggle to be kind to other people even in this group.

I saw you struggle to be patient. I saw your eyebrow go up and the anger start, and then I saw you struggling with both hands to bring the eyebrow down. I saw you struggling to be generous. I saw you struggle to help other people in physical ways. I saw you in bursts of devotion agree to put crazy people in your homes for a few weeks and it stretched into a few months, and I saw you struggle with that. I saw you struggle to give away things. I saw many times sweet students here held something they really wanted in their hands, and I saw them struggle to put their hands out and give it to another person.

I learned to identify what I call a "book decision." Many people are keeping the practice of a diary, a spiritual diary, to every few hours track their vows: "How am I doing?" At the end of each entry we are supposed to write a little "to do." Like "give the person I really don't like my favorite thing." And you will spot these events in the class from time to time. Two students you know who had tension, and one is giving the other this incredibly beautiful thing, and you say, "That was a book decision."

But this is pure Buddhist practice. This is what we are here to do. It was wonderful to watch. It's all artificial. It's all strained. It's all with a great deal of tension. The person who knows you don't like them is looking under the thing: "Is there a bomb or something?"

And I could watch you, like a television, to see the struggle to keep your holy bodhisattva vows, your kindness vows. I watched the ordained people struggle to keep the *pratimoksha* vows in a country where everything goes the other way. I watch everyone struggle to do their meditations. I watched you struggle to educate yourselves. You have much to dedicate. I think there are many physical good deeds we have done, but the main ones are the inner struggles to be kind to other people. And it's obvious that it's a struggle. But it is the most beautiful thing in the world to see a person struggling to be good.

And so you kept your vows well. You learned your vows. There are very few Buddhists in history who have learned their vows. *Yama, niyama dompa and damtsik.* How to restrain our impulses. How to try to be kind to others and not selfish.

I've seen you struggle with the secret vows. I've seen you struggle with the secret teachings. They are the hardest. A vow is kept or broken in a split second of doubt or faith. I saw you struggle deeply with those vows. I've seen you struggle, like all disciples struggle, with the vows that relate to a teacher. But try to remember that every struggle you've had—and those of us in retreat, twenty four hours a day, we have nothing else to do but struggle with our inner selves—every tiny struggle is an intense good karma. To flow with your natural selfishness is easy and it destroys the world. To struggle, try to turn yourself into a good person, is intense good karma. Every struggle that you've had is beautiful.

Lastly I'd like to mention, and then we'll take a break, I have watched you educate yourselves, train yourselves. I want to remind you about that good karma. It is the ultimate good karma to struggle to learn about emptiness, to struggle to learn about karma. When you can't remember any good karma you have done, here's a list:

You've studied the Perfection of Wisdom, the holy teachings of the Second Turning of the Wheel, in depth. You've studied *lamrim*, the great teachings on the Path to Enlightenment, in depth. You've studied three or four different *lamrim*s. You've studied the complete instructions on how to meditate from the ancient texts of India, *Bhavanakrama, Kamalashila*. Very few people have had those two or three lineages. In ancient Tibet it was a great honor; it was incredibly rare to have even one of those teachings.

You have studied the ancient texts, *Pramanavarttika* by Dharmakirti, on how to establish past and future lives. You studied extensively from the *Abhidharma* by

Master Vasubandhu—how karma works exactly. You have had that lineage. Very, very few people, even in Tibet, received even one of those lineages. You have received those five or six.

You have received the lineage of the Diamond Cutter Sutra, perhaps the greatest teaching ever given on emptiness. Your karma created the only commentary in Tibet to be found a few months before your classes began. After that you studied the whole bodhisattva vow teachings of Master Asanga and Lord Buddha, from, oh, seventeen, eighteen centuries ago for Master Asanga, and two and half thousand years ago for Lord Buddha. You have had the karma to enter a two-and-a-half-thousand-year lineage.

It's not an exaggeration to say you are one in a million or five million people. You have the karma to have drunk from those lineages. Maybe one out of a hundred monks in Tibet would have even had two or three.

Then you had the karma to study the ancient teachings on death—what happens to people afterwards, where they go, why—from Master Vasubandhu, seventeen centuries ago. Then you entered the lineage of Vinaya instructions. You received the lineage of Je Tsongkapa's teachings on Vinaya, and you entered the lineage of Gunaprabha—Master Gunaprabha—from fifteen hundred years ago.

After that, you received the entire lineage of Master Shantideva, *The Bodhisattva's Way of Life*. After that, you received the most precious lineage of Master Dharmakirti on how to reason. This is the key to all meditation and this is the key to see emptiness. After that, you entered the lineage of *lojong*, the ancient teachings on kindness from the very first Tibetan lamas.

After that, you entered the lineage of *drange*, how to distinguish between what the Buddha really meant and what he didn't really mean. You mastered the Mind-Only school. Very few people in history have heard those teachings. You heard, you got the lineage of Heart Sutra. You studied the different types of mandalas.

And due to the intense kindness of holy Lama Khen Rinpoche, many people here have been granted entry into the lineage of the secret teachings. There are people here who studied those secret teachings, and even more advanced versions, with the head of the Tantric College, Geshe Trinley Tobgyey. Those people studied the secret teachings of Naropa.

There are people here who were granted teachings by holy Lama Geshe Thubten Rinchen. In five hundred years of existence of Sera monastery, a group of foreigners entered the monastery—I think the first time, about fifteen of you; later about eighty people—and were granted in the main temple permission to receive the lineages of *drange* from the greatest master in the world of that subject, and the Mind-Only school.

I can't describe to you how rare that was. That was the first time since Je Tsongkapa that a group of foreigners was allowed to study those subjects in Sera. Many of you were present when the head of the Tantric College of *Gyutu*, Geshe Tenzin Sherab, taught to our classes in New York. So I think in the world there are probably only maybe a hundred people who have been instructed by both heads of the great Tantric Colleges of Tibet. You are among them.

Many of you have had teachings from the greatest lama to bring Buddhism into the other countries of the world. This is Lama Zopa. Needless to say, almost everyone here, or many people, have had the chance to study, listen to His Holiness the Dalai Lama. He will certainly go down as the greatest Dalai Lama. To teach for his whole life around the world, to devote every hour of his life to others, to be chosen at the age of three and to win a Nobel prize. You have received more holy lineages than anyone in Tibet ever did. Whenever you are feeling down, whenever you think your practice isn't so hot, try to imagine the immense good karma you have created.

Those lineages reached this country only through the kindness of one being, it's holy Lama, Khen Rinpoche. You don't understand that there's no lama like him in all of the monasteries, because he's the only one you've had the contact with.

Also many of you have studied, were there when Gyalrong Khensur Rinpoche taught our monks and nuns and other people about our vows. You have received the vows from the greatest Vinaya master in the world. Many of you were there; we received teachings from Khombo Khensur Rinpoche, Jampa Donyo. This lama helped to save all the Sanskrit texts that we have. He spent twelve years in Varanasi struggling to save the ancient, ancient books. He taught you.

Many of you took teachings from Pomra Khensur, Geshe Losang Ngudrup, who has passed from this world. He taught us *lamrim*. Many of you heard teachings from holy Lama Geshe Lobsang Thardo, perhaps the greatest master of guru yoga in this world.

Some of you had teachings from Tenzin Trinlay Rinpoche, ancient master of the Vajra Yogini lineages, disguised as a lay man just coming through New York. And many other lineages.

When you think you're not so special, when you try to think of something to dedicate, I can't describe to you what karma you must have, and what new karma you have created. To meet an abbot of a Tantric College in Tibet was a rare honor. People would walk to Lhasa from Kham, in the Munlam festival, to see the Dalai Lama's head pass by at the top of the crowd. No one received such teachings. You must be special. You must be something very special. You must have some special mission. These holy beings must have something in mind for you to do. They wouldn't come to you otherwise. You can't force the Dalai Lama to teach you.

So remember those good karmas. You have excellent practice. You have extraordinary personal practice, each one of you. You have to think about it, crystallize that good karma, and send it to other people's hearts tonight.

We'll take a break. Please enjoy the refreshments.

[Break]

So if everyone here has got so many beautiful karmic seeds in their heart to send to others' hearts, then who to send them to exactly? This is what Master Shantideva's chapter is all about. It's like a Christmas list. It's like Santa Claus' list of where to go. And it's a beautiful suggestion list of where to send your good karmas.

Yesterday we spoke about the verses that mainly relate to people who are just entering a spiritual path. Now today there will be suggestions from this holy master about where to send them for people who are already on a spiritual path. And I'd like to ask that one of those sweet people who are reading the verses read the first verse.

John Stilwell:

(42) **May places of spiritual learning thrive,**
Filled with people reading sacred books,

> And singing them out loud as well.
> May communities of spiritual practitioners
> Live always in harmony, and may they achieve
> The high goals for which they live together.

In the first half of the verse, Master Shantideva is saying, "send your good karmas to all the spiritual centers in the world." I think here especially you can see it as ripples going out from your heart. You drop your good karma of putting up with that person next to you this afternoon into your heart, and then it starts to spread.

First it hits all the sweet spiritual learning centers that we are close to—for example, Diamond Mountain retreat center—and you send it to the hearts of all who are working to create this place. And then a little bit wider and you hit ACI New York and pray for all the people who are working and studying there. Send them your good karma. Send it to their hearts, especially the director. It's a hard job. I'm glad *he's* director.

Then you can send it to Godstow retreat center in Connecticut. Then you can send it to the people working so hard to save the ancient books of Tibet, the Asian Classics Input Project people. They are all over the world. Send some to their sweet director and the two or three close people who are working with him.

There's a Geshe in Sera who has devoted much of his life to organizing the work there. He needs a lot of good karma. It's a hard job. There are many refugees working, a large number of them poor women, in Tibetan refugee villages. And send them your good karma. There are young scholars for that in Russia and Mongolia. They are often lonely; they have a hard time in a foreign country. Send them your good karma. Pray for their success.

Of course we should send good karmas to holy Lama Khen Rinpoche's devoted students in New Jersey and Washington and other places, who have devoted their whole lives to assure that the written lineage and spoken lineage and practice in their own hearts will be spread.

Then I think it's important to send it to centers like Vajrapani Institute or Land of Medicine Buddha or other many centers of holy Lama Zopa Rinpoche. Each one of these places is very, very precious. There are too few places in the world where you can learn these things. If it's true that they can save a human life, if it's true that they can prevent pain for millions of people, there are too few [such places] in the world. We have to send our good karmas to all of them, all the lineages of Buddhism in this country.

We tend to foolishly, stupidly, ignorantly, violently put down other centers of other traditions, other faiths. It's like demanding that there be only one hospital in Arizona. It's incredibly stupid and foolish. Each hospital has a role. Each small medical center has a role. If one person who is hurt can go to that place, it should exist and we should send it our good wishes and good karma.

And so we must send our good karma not only to the Buddhist centers but all of the religious centers in our country and other countries. There's no church, or synagogue, or temple which exists if someone doesn't benefit from it. They will just disappear and close. Therefore, if they are open and people are going there, it's important that they stay open, like a hospital. It's so foolish to wish that hospitals be destroyed or that people should only come to our hospital. So we should work as hard as we can to support the other spiritual centers of the world, of every faith, because they suit the needs of some sick person.

And as we said yesterday, in spiritual centers, especially of a new kind of religion in a country like here, you find groups of very stubborn people. You wouldn't be here if you weren't stubborn. And so naturally we rub each other the wrong way sometimes. And we have to try to send karma ahead to prevent those kinds of problems.

Geshe Ngawang Dhargyey, holy lama who has passed from this world, who blessed Australia and New Zealand with his teachings especially, he used to hold up a single pencil in the class in India and break it. And then he would take about fifteen pencils and hold it up and ask if any student wished to come and try to break it, together. And he said, "Your spiritual life is like that. If you can find friends who have the same goals, you can stay close to each other, support each other."

And so it's important that people should come together and work together. It makes you stronger. Send your special wishes to communities of spiritual people who are working towards similar goals. I think it's especially important for all of us to send our good karma to the Tibetan monasteries and centers in Tibet and India. The ones in Tibet are struggling. There's a grand revival happening. They have the special motivation of people who are endangered by the circumstances there. The same in Mongolia.

And, I think, especially important to send our good karmas to Sera monastery, and Sera Mey in particular, because of the incredible kindness she has given to us by sending us holy Lama Khen Rinpoche. Those places will continue to produce people like Rinpoche for future generations. We have to work very hard to help them physically and send them our good karmas.

So please, very important, every church, every temple, every mosque in this world is contributing to the happiness of people. We have to pray that they stay for a long time.

It mentions studying books, reading them and singing them. We have a choice. We can read fifty books, or you can get deeply into one book. You can spend a year on fifty books, or you can spend a year on one special book. Maybe memorize that book. Sing it out loud when you can. Master Shantideva is sending you a small suggestion. I think it's a beautiful idea. Those of you who have a *dakkye* practice, a *sadhana*, I think especially he's encouraging you to memorize it. Put it in your mind. If you die tomorrow, it will go with you. Next verse please.

Edie Roach:

(43) **May all those who have ever taken**
The vows of a monk come to master
The arts of solitude,
Throwing off every kind of distraction,
Gradually refining their minds,
Learning perfect meditation.

Master Shantideva begins to pray for ordained people. But in our context, it refers to anyone who is trying to do a spiritual practice. Not just monks or nuns, but anyone here, for example, who's struggling to keep a spiritual practice. He says, "May they learn the arts of solitude." I know that you know there are two kinds of solitude. One is physical. You give your credit card debt bills to the caretakers and the director and you go stay in a yurt. Sorry. *[Laughs.]* And you achieve physical solitude.

It's much more difficult to achieve inner solitude. All the scriptures say that. If you could sit in an office in New York City and maintain your level of samadhi, your concentration, your pure heart, in the midst of chaos, then you have real solitude. Physical solitude is fragile. It's hard to keep those perfect circumstances, like we have. But if you develop inner solitude, you could take it anywhere.

I sometimes worry that some people seek physical solitude and then they almost become weaker in their ability to maintain inner solitude under very difficult circumstances. I think those of you who are in difficult jobs, difficult family situations that place difficult demands on you, have a great opportunity to develop inner solitude. And it doesn't matter then where you go. But also if you truly wish to see emptiness, if you truly wish to achieve high states of meditation, it's very useful, occasionally, or often as you get older, to go into deep physical solitude.

He says, "May they be released from distractions." And those are just mainly, in Master Shantideva, he's talking about the distraction of thinking about yourself and forgetting others. Then you can reach deep states of meditation. It's a very beautiful thing that people in this group are doing so many deep retreats. We don't know precisely, but we have kinds of information that people are doing deep retreats, and this is a very wonderful thing. I hope you will continue it. OK, next verse.

Fran Dayan:

(44) **May nuns forever find support**
For their physical needs, and live lives free
Of conflict or any outside threat.
May every person who's ever become
Ordained conduct themselves
Perfectly in their moral code.

Then it's a special prayer for nuns. But it can refer I think to all of us. In ancient times it was very difficult for nuns to find support. I think it continues today. I'm very proud of the fact that almost all, or maybe all of the retreatants are women. It's a very great step. I think it's a great example for the future. And I think it's great that so many people have given us support.

Then Master Shantideva prays that they would live in harmony. We mentioned yesterday women have to be even more stubborn to do deep spiritual practice, because of the ancient prejudices of our world. And so there are even more stubborn people put together, and more potential for disharmony. There are ancient books from India and Tibet on removing disharmony from groups. I think that means there must have been disharmony. And it's a very terrible thing.

Many lamas have mentioned to me that of all the things we should watch out for the worst is disharmony within a group. You have to set aside your personal wishes, you have to set aside your opinions sometimes, when it's necessary to maintain the harmony. There's nothing that turns off young students more than seeing disharmony of those people who have been trained so well.

Then Master Shantideva says, "May the women practitioners be free from outside threats." It's been a tradition, a cruel tradition throughout history, if an army came through a country, to attack the convents and the nunneries especially. They were vulnerable. And it continues to happen, in Tibet for example. And so we pray that they not be hurt by outside threats.

Then Master Shantideva sends his energy to all people with vows. It's one thing to decide not to harm other people and animals, not to kill them for example. It's much more powerful if you commit yourself not to do it, formally, before a high lama like His Holiness or Khen Rinpoche. And Master Shantideva is saying, "All those people who have made a commitment like that, I send them my good karma. May they have the strength to keep those commitments they made."

Vilma Staiano:
**(45)   And may any of those who may have ever
Broken this code regret what they've done,
And always work to clean the karma.
May they then return to a higher birth,
And in their new life never see
Their spiritual discipline fail again.**

[Laughs.] A lot of Geshes today.

It's more powerful to commit yourself not to do a wrong thing, and it's more powerful if you break that commitment than if you hadn't made that commitment.

There's a great lama, Lord Atisha, who helped bring Buddhism to Tibet from India. He said, "My vows are like the weather. My monk's vows, I've broken almost none of them, like a tiny drip from a faucet. My bodhisattva vows, my vows to be kind to others, I break pretty frequently, like a steady soft rain. And my tantric vows, which you can break in a single instant of negative thoughts towards a holy being, I have broken like a wild thunderstorm." He used to carry around a small stupa, a small image, and stop all day long and pray that the bad karma of just thinking something wrong shouldn't grow.

And so I think we are similar. I think we are fortunate to have had great lamas. We understand our vows. We are special in that way. But the mental ones especially are so hard to keep. And so send your good karma.

And here I introduce a new idea. Those of you who have done *tong-len*—the practice of giving and taking with your breathing—you know that you can send energy ahead into the future to help yourself also. You can send your good karma to yourself tomorrow or next week or next year. And send your good karma ahead, your good karma from maybe the first days of your spiritual life when you turned away from the pain of this world, and send it ahead to yourself and say, "This is energy shipment from me now to me future. I hope it helps you to keep your vows."

Then Master Shantideva does what we call a *mayin gak* in Buddhist logic. He makes one statement by saying something else. He says, "I hope they can come back to a higher life and keep their vows better in the future."

He's saying that it's very dangerous to break your commitments. It can take you to terrible states of physical and mental misery. And he's trying to send energy to those people who have broken their commitments. You have also learned carefully how to clean bad karma, and it's important to keep doing that practice, especially with the fire.

I think lastly I'd like to tell you—on this verse, don't get your hopes up—we noticed something in our *sojong* rituals together. *Sojong* ritual, if you don't know, is a group ritual to admit to each other the things we've done wrong, openly, and to encourage and support each other to improve in the future.

And so sometimes what we've been doing when we meet, which is not the whole group, and only during break months: we keep our book, diary, during the day. We stop six times during the day; we check one of our vows and see if we have broken it or if we've done very well with it. And then every two weeks, which was yesterday, for example, on the full moon, we take that diary and we snip out some of the hits and some of the—what do you call—disasters. Then we share them with each other, and then at the end of the ritual we burn them all. The good ones go up in smoke and send energy to the planet; the bad ones are destroyed.

But something interesting happened. We began to notice that some of us were confessing for others. We would share a written entry from our diary, and it would say, "I managed to stay patient while Retreatant B was being such an asshole, when they broke their vows so terribly." And then Retreatant B saw it and they said, "This is lucky. You're doing my *sojong* for me."

So I think it's important. The only person who can keep your vows is you. And the only person who can keep other people's vows is them. We don't have to keep theirs for them.

You know there are secret vows. If there are secret vows that you know about, I think it's logical to assume there maybe secret vows we don't know about, that we haven't heard about yet. And so we have to be very careful with this dedication, I believe. Send your good karma to those who seem to have broken their vows, but never forget to say "seem." "Seems like that to me." Because we never really know. And I think it's a tendency for all of us. Okay, next.

Allison Jucha:
(46) **May every sage who lives in this world**
Find the honor due to them, and always be offered
The food and other needs they request.
May they always take care that their hearts are pure,
And may they earn a good name that spreads
Throughout the entire world.

This is a special dedication of good karma for sages, could be yogis or great meditators or lamas. But at some point in a person's spiritual life they may, I think you can call it, "turn professional." And there's a change in the way you live.

Some teachers follow the path of dedicating their whole time to externally teaching others in an obvious way, and then they become dependent on the kindness of others for their support. In ancient India the word for monk was *bhikshu*, and *bhikshu* means "to eat" but it also means "to beg for your food." And so it's a prayer that those who've chosen that path will get all the support that they need. And it's sending karma.

You wouldn't guess how much, frankly, financial trouble great lamas have had, and have. His Holiness the Dalai Lama has tremendous debts because he's supporting hundreds and hundreds of monks. He is, frankly, in very difficult financial situations constantly. Holy Lama Khen Rinpoche, we told him, "Don't worry, Rinpoche. We'll give you $115 a month." Six months out of the year we couldn't do it. He never said a word. He never complained.

His refrigerator was often empty. I can remember a day when he said, "Go to the refrigerator. Give the food and make tea for all the students."

I said, "Rinpoche, there's nothing there. There's a quart of milk." He said, "Bring the quart of milk and make tea and give it to everyone." Then he didn't have anything for himself.

So we have to pray that people like that always have enough support. But when you begin to accept support from others it comes with a heavy karmic responsibility. This is very serious in the Vinaya. It's described. The karma of support which others have given you so you can practice is extremely dangerous. To waste another person's precious life by not using that support properly is very, very powerful bad karma. And I also especially encourage the retreatants here. We can't waste a single drop of food. We can't demand anything that we don't desperately need. We can't complain about any of the circumstances, ever. It's extremely bad karma.

And so Master Shantideva is saying, "May those people who get support, like we are, conduct themselves in a way which would make the people proud who are supporting them." Next verse please.

Nancy Carin:

(47)   **May none of these people ever again**
           Undergo the pain of the lower realms;

> **In strength beyond the strength of gods**
> **May they quickly win the state**
> **Of a fully Enlightened One**
> **Without the slightest hardship.**

[Laughs.] Master Shantideva's praying—this is a sum up—all the people who are devoted to a spiritual path should have good physical and mental health for the whole time that they are reaching Enlightenment. They should have strong, healthy bodies, strong, healthy minds, until the day they reach Enlightenment. And so it's sort of a summary verse. Next verse please.

Kimberly Anderson:

> **(48) May every suffering being there is**
> **Make offerings over and over again**
> **To every Enlightened Being there is.**
> **And may the Enlightened Ones enjoy**
> **Forever what we have offered them,**
> **In infinite waves of bliss.**

I have trouble with offering, I tell you honestly. I see lamas like holy Lama Zopa Rinpoche or Khen Rinpoche set out extraordinary offerings all over their rooms, sometimes thousands of offerings around the house. And I have difficulty with that. I have trouble, I think, imagining a Buddha will come down and drink a bowl of water or eat a cookie the way that Santa Claus would take the milk and the cookies. I have trouble with it mentally.

But I think it's important for us to understand that's not what happens when we make an offering. We offer physical objects to our teachers and to Holy Beings. If the teacher is a true yogi practitioner, they have absolutely no need for almost anything we can offer them. A real yogi teacher sees another possession in their room as a new enemy. It's just trouble, one more thing to disturb my meditation. They get rid of it as soon as they can.

There's a beautiful story. You know: Student A goes to Lama Zopa Rinpoche, gives him a priceless rosary. Goes and sits down in the reception room. Student B goes in for his blessing. Student B comes out wearing the rosary. True story. Repeated over and over.

But the offering has been completed, and the offering is perfect. You have offered to your lama or Holy Beings something that means a lot to you. The minute you thought to offer it, it was offered. The minute you thought about offering the water bowl or the piece of fruit or the flower on the altar, countless Buddhas in countless parts of the universe were struck with countless waves of bliss. You should know that. It's true. Don't be discouraged or think that offering is silly.

I had students bitterly complain to me that they saw another student wearing a sweater they gave me. It means you don't understand the offering. The minute you decide to give, the minute you put out your arms to offer the thing, countless Enlightened Beings are overwhelmed with extraordinary bliss and emptiness perceptions. Does it mean they don't have bliss before? Of course not. Does it mean you gave them more bliss than they had before? Of course not. It's for us. It's that we have triggered more bliss in them and it's an extraordinary good karma. So Master Shantideva is saying whenever any single person in this room offers even a little bowl of water, may every Holy Being be overcome with infinite waves of bliss and emptiness. Next verse.

Doug Veenhof:

(49) **May every plan there is in the heart**
Of every bodhisattva to help
Every living being come true.
May everyone get every single thing
That the Enlightened Ones who shelter us
Have in mind for us to get.

I was thinking about this verse this morning. I used to work for a carpenter in the summertime in college. He was a beautiful, extraordinary man named Otto. He was very small and old. He smoked a pipe. He had an old Kansas hat on. And he was such a beautiful man. And he would come up and say, "Hey you, young feller. Take those two-by-fours there and nail 'em together like this." And I'd nail them together. And I would break my watch off because my aim was so poor.

He told me one day, "I can make a carpenter out of your brother Geoff, but you're hopeless." And he would just set me to the stupid work, and I'd nail a couple of boards together, and then three days later he'd say, "Where's them boards?" And I'd go get the boards. And then he'd adjust them and put them into the structure of this new house. And I had no idea what the house would look like. I didn't know what he was asking me to do. He had the whole house in his mind. And he would—three days and four days ahead, to make me busy—he would tell me to nail some things together. He has a vision of this whole house. He knows every nail that's going to be going into this house. And I don't have the slightest clue; I just nail them together.

Bodhisattvas are like that. They are working on a totally different level. We can't, people can't even imagine what bodhisattvas have in mind. They can't imagine the extent of their vision. They are truly working on a universal level. They see things that will not happen for hundreds or thousands or perhaps even millions of years.

I'm not talking about Buddhas. I'm talking about a bodhisattva who has seen emptiness. They have a special knowledge of the master plan. They see the whole house. When they ask us to do a small thing—"Nail them boards together"—we have to do it. They have a master plan. They have a plan we could never imagine.

And so Master Shantideva is saying, "I pray that whatever plans these bodhisattvas have, they should come true. And people who are asked to contribute and nail boards together for the master house, they should try to do it happily and understand that a larger thing is happening."

With Buddhas it's even beyond that—future, past, for all time, is compressed into a single point. They see everything that will ever happen and that has ever happened, everywhere, in a single instant. And so it's very powerful to send them your good karma. Can you imagine how big your seeds will get if you just make a simple, little prayer: "May the Enlightened Beings' wishes be fulfilled, their plans."

For them, a million years is nothing. *Jneyam alpam.* The world is reduced to water, a rain puddle for them. So in this verse, when you try to practice, send your good karma that the master plans of these Beings be realized. Next verse please.

Rebecca Vinacour:

(50)   May those who follow the lower paths
Of self-made awakened ones, and listeners,
Attain the happiness they seek.

Those of you who know Buddhist philosophy, "self-made Buddha" is a code word for practitioners who are very advanced but don't have compassion—ultimate compassion—yet. And "listeners" is the same. These are code words for high practitioners, very advanced yogis and meditators, but they don't yet grasp—they haven't directly experienced—the extraordinary wish to act on a universal level for all beings. And so it's almost, if you notice, the verse is very short. Master Shantideva is making a frank put-down of these people. He doesn't even give them a whole verse. He gives them half a verse. He says, "Good luck, guys." But the very fact that it's such a short verse is a statement. The fact that it is the only verse in the whole chapter which is cut into half, it's a half a verse, is an implicit prayer that you and I should never fall into that kind of attitude. Next verse.

Elizabeth Prather:
(51) **And may we, through the kindness**
Of Gentle Voice, remember in life after life
Who we are and what we practice,
Rejecting the worldly way of life
Again and again, until the day
We reach the level called Intense Joy.

If you notice, this is the first verse where it changes to "we." All the other verses, almost, have been "them." Master Shantideva is saying, "Take your good karmas and send them to your future self. Take your good karmas and ship them to yourself."

For what? To reach "Intense Joy."

What's "Intense Joy"?

"Intense Joy" is a code word. It's the Sanskrit name—*pramudita*—for the first level of a bodhisattva. This is the name for the first of the ten bodhisattva levels. You reach "Intense Joy," the level called "Intense Joy," when you see emptiness for the first time. You step on that level in the first millisecond that you have seen emptiness with the wish to help every single living creature in the universe in your heart. And at that moment you see them all, you see every one of them in a yogic perception, in a deep meditative direct perception of every living creature in the entire universe.

Each of us, if you haven't come there already, you can reach that place. You have to try. It's why we are here. It's why all of these teachings are going on. It's the purpose for their retreat. It's the purpose for our very lives. All of us, if you haven't reached this place, must try. What can stop you from reaching this place? The worst thing is if you forget why you should reach it. And that's because we have to serve others.

I mentioned earlier today some of the terrible pain that I know has happened actually to people here. You have to keep that in mind. You can't ever forget it. We are only here to stop that pain for every one of us. And so send your good karma ahead into the future. By the blessings of Gentle Voice—a name for Manjushri, the bodhisattva or the deity who represents the direct perception of emptiness. And may we never forget why we are here. It's the only reason we are all working so hard. Everything we do is to reach the level of Intense Joy. Send your good karmas ahead to yourself and others, if they haven't reached this level that they should reach this Intense Joy.

Now you have an opportunity to reach the level of intense joy of refreshments. And please have another short break. We don't have much after that.

[Break]

[Laughs.] OK. I'm sorry it goes on a little long. I'd like to finish the whole chapter. Not tonight. *[Laughs.]*

But also we like to be with you. We miss you very much. It means a lot to us that you come. And I think all of us sort of like to drag it on so we can be close to you. We really miss you a lot. OK, next verse please.

Batbold Baast:
(52)   May we gain the mystic ability
To live off even the poorest of food,
Growing ever more strong and healthy.
In all our lives may we win the wealth
Of learning to live in solitude
With nothing more than barest needs.

[Laughs.] Wow. OK. It's very simple verse. As we start to work more and more for other people, there should be a corresponding shrinking of our own needs. And it's a wonderful experience, even if you can do it a little bit. But as your attitude shifts more from selfishness to giving for others, say giving to others, then naturally your own needs should start to shrink. And the combination—I think Master Shantideva is specifically saying—after you've seen emptiness, after you've reached Intense Joy, is that you start to change your body in the years after that. Your life begins to change. Especially if you're trying to practice the secret teachings, then your own needs begin to shrink drastically.

On a moral level you should use less of the world's resources, and on a physical level your body needs less food, less sleep. Your needs begin to shrink because you are seeing the first stages of your body's transformation into light. And on a very gross level, people like us should begin to have less impact on our Earth. We should begin to use less of her resources.

I'm not a great ecologist, but living here for the last few years, I think all of us retreatants have begun to appreciate deeply the wilderness and the wildlife, the other people who share our world. We have become close friends and companions to the local creatures. They eat with us often. They will even come to the door and wait for us, try to catch our attention. All sorts of wonderful creatures. And we begin to sense the need to share the Earth with them in a deep way.

And I think as spiritual practitioners, as our physical needs should shrink as we serve others, we should and we do become more sensitive to the fact that every time we use a single object—food or material object—that we don't really need, every time we eat something that we don't really need, we are taking things away from the Earth and from other creatures and from our future children and grandchildren. And so this verse is, I think, a very beautiful statement of simplifying our needs so we can serve others. Next verse.

Susan McKenna:

(54) **We are working to achieve the goals
Of all the living things there are
In every corner of this universe;
And so by this power may we learn to do
Every single one of the things**

That Gentle Voice is able to do.

[Laughs.] It's a prayer, sending energy to ourselves in the future, that we should learn to act like Manjushri himself. Mainly the power to see emptiness directly. May we learn to see that. Send power ahead to yourself. And also to act in secret ways, to act around the world in secret ways. Next verse.

Yuri Talalaev:

(55) **And may we decide that we will stay**
To work to clear away the pain
Of every living being there is
Until the last day of this
Universe; until the very last
Suffering creature is changed.

It's a prayer that we learn to take responsibility for everyone else. And it begins with just the work you are doing anywhere. For example, if there's a teaching like this then you stick around after it's over. We used to serve Holy Lama during the retreats in New Jersey. They used to be ten days long. And many people would come. And on Sunday afternoon there'd be a small tornado of cars leaving, and suddenly the entire grounds of the temple and the house were empty of people and full of garbage and work to do, clean up. And it's a kind of attitude that begins with small things like that.

Will you be there the day after the teaching, offering to help people clean up and put things away? Will you wait around until the real end of the virtue? And then it expands on a greater level. Are you willing to make a commitment to stay as long as it takes to help the last person through the door?

Many of you know, who have studied deeply, that it's not true that bodhisattvas must stay and suffer until the last person is through the door of enlightenment. It works the other way around. A bodhisattva's job is to get enlightened immediately, go to nirvana and highest enlightenment as fast as you can, because then you can emanate countless bodies and help other people in trillions more ways than you can if you wait. So it's not correct, the rumor that bodhisattvas choose to stay in the suffering world until every other person is gone beyond—it's the opposite. But we have to have the attitude that we would be willing to stay and suffer if we had to, to help others. In actuality, your job is very exciting. You have to get to total bliss quickly so you can really help others. This is just as statement of the attitude that you should have that you will work for others' sake. You will think of others first.

There are many students—and I do it myself—who say we're working for all living beings, and then when there's only one donut left in the box we eat it ourselves. We do that. It's a sign. It's an indication. It's a danger signal that we don't have bodhisattva's attitude. It starts with small things. You can't claim to be a bodhisattva or studying bodhisattva's way of life if you can't give away a cup of tea or the last donut. We have to start with those things. We have to start with small things. And give them away to other people. Next verse.

Ben Brewer:

(56)   **May every single pain that is coming**
To any single being there is
Ripen now upon me instead.
May the great community of bodhisattvas
Go forth and spread through all the world,
To work for the happiness of all.

This is an ancient practice of trying to take other people's bad karma away from them and swallow it ourselves. It's so important, I'd like to leave it, if you don't mind, for tomorrow. What was the second half?
"May the great community of bodhisattvas…"

Oh, OK. There's a beautiful Sanskrit verse. Let's see if I can remember. *Kanda itva kala dandam brahmande vicaranti.* It means—"*kanda itva*" means "those Holy Beings who are walking around on this planet in disguise, among the mass of people." In the dakkye, it starts, *Ji nye dorje kandroma*, "however many you may be, I don't know."

Kala dandam means, "*kala*" means "time" but it's a word for the Lord of Death. "*Dandam*" means "a club," "a stick." It means, "those who have clubbed death to death." It's a beautiful word, *kala dandam*. "Those who have murdered death," because they have moved beyond this kind of body, they have entered a state beyond death. It is the goal of all of us, and to take other people there. *Brahmande* means "the egg of Brahma." It's a word for the universe. *Vicarantite* means "those who wander around the world in disguise helping the rest of us."

And Master Shantideva's prayer is the same: "I send the energy of writing this holy book, *Bodhisattvacaryavattara*, I send it to all those secret agents, bodhisattvas, who are all over the place. May you continue to wander through our world and help people secretly." Next verse.

John McCluskey:

(57) **The teachings of the Enlightened Ones**
Are the one medicine that can cure
The great sickness of living kind.
They are the one ultimate source
Of every form of happiness.
And so by this power may the teachings remain
Long upon this planet, with all the support
They require, and all the respect they deserve.

Master Shantideva is praying that the single medicine for all suffering should remain in this world, the teachings of the Enlightened Ones. It boils down to one thing: Serve other people. Take care of other people. Take care of other people. It's the whole teaching in that one sentence: take care of other people. If people continue to take care of others, then the teachings of all religions are staying on this planet. And they are the one medicine for all pain in this world. And anything that contributes to keeping that idea in this world, send your good karma to that. Next verse.

Ven. Elly van der Pas:

(58) **And lastly do I bow myself**
Down to the One with a Gentle Voice,
The One who has been kind enough
To teach me the ways of virtue;
Thus last do I bow myself down
To the One who was kind enough
To raise me up from childhood:

**I bow to You,
My Spiritual Guide.**

In the actual chapter, this is the final verse—I've rearranged the verses for this teaching. We all come to our teachers like children, small children. I remember, I think the first day I came to holy Lama Khen Rinpoche. I was, I think, twenty-two. And one of his senior students sat me down and said, "I'll be honest with you. It's a lot more trouble to have you here than not to have you here. It will be more trouble for Rinpoche." He was called "Geshe-la" at the time. "Your very presence here is trouble for Rinpoche."

I was very new. I was sort of blown away. And I went home to my little room and I thought about it. And I thought, "I'm going to try not to be trouble." But I was. And I still am. And it's hard; it's hard to bring up a student. It's a lot of pain. It's a lot of work. It's not easy—you can't finish this in a year or two. It takes a lifetime. And that relationship remains for many lifetimes. And in a sense our teachers have taken us like a child in a basket left at the door. And they take responsibility for us. And we fight them. We struggle against them. We can't listen to them. If we could, we wouldn't need them. It's true. It's by definition: *rang gi tsennyi kyi druppa*. We don't know enough to even be a good student. That's why we're a student.

And so the last verse is a prayer, sending whatever little good karma we have to our teachers. "I'm sorry for being such a difficult case. And I pray that you will stay with me. I pray that all my teachers, my many teachers here, will not give up on me. I pray that you will continue to try to guide me, even when I'm crazy and I'm fighting you. Even when I don't listen to you. Even when I refuse to see who you are."

Third Day:
Saturday, March 30, 2002

Let's meditate for a few minutes.

We were speaking about Jesus. He had been taken tied, his hands tied behind his back, to the fortress: Antonia Fortress of the Roman Empire's troops. And the Roman governor—military governor—has been asked to decide on his case. He must be considered important if the governor, on the day before the biggest holiday of the year, has agreed to hear his case specially. Pontius Pilate has questioned him and then gone back outside to the people assembled there the religious authorities who have accused Jesus. And he says, "I don't find any fault in this good man."

Actually Pontius Pilate is thinking hard. He knows Jesus has a lot of support among the poor people especially, and if he kills him with thousands of extra strong Jewish people in the city for the holiday, there could be a major uprising. On the other hand if he doesn't kill him, then the Council of Elders who control the people also will start to work against him. And so he's looking for a way out. And people in the crowd cry out, "He's not a good man; he's been stirring up the people all the way from Galilee in the north down to Jerusalem."

Pilate says, "Galilee? He's from Galilee?"

The people say, "Yes."

He says, "Ah, not my jurisdiction." *[Laughter in audience.]*

Herod the Great, the king who died shortly after Jesus was born, was incredibly cruel and powerful. He actually killed most of his own family, because he became very paranoid in his old age. He's also the one who killed all the young boys in the area where Jesus was born, because he had spoken to the three kings, the wise men, and received information that a king might be born to compete with him. He had two surviving sons. One is called Herod Antipas. One is Herod Philip. The Roman emperor believes in Herod's power so much that he has allowed Herod to pass the kingdom on by inheritance, and it has been split into four parts. Herod Antipas controls the north, Galilee included. Herod Philip controls the northeast, to the east of the Jordan River. A son named Archalaus was given the jewel, Jerusalem and Judea, the large central province. And a sister was given some small lands on the ocean and near Jerusalem.

Archalaus was such a cruel ruler that he was shortly overthrown by the Jewish people, especially in Jerusalem, and the Romans have sent a military governor named Pontius Pilate to take his place. Bad luck or good luck for Jesus, Herod Antipas is in town for the holidays. He has a separate huge palace on the western side of the city. And so Pontius Pilate makes a quick decision to send Jesus to Herod Antipas, the king of Galilee.

This is a very bad turn of events. Herod Antipas has inherited the cruelty of his father. He has taken his brother's own wife—Herod Philip's wife—and committed adultery with her and is living with her in his palace. There's a holy man from the desert, named John, who baptizes many people, so they call him John the Baptist. He criticizes the king openly for his misconduct. John lives in the desert. He's like a crazy man. He dresses in the skins of wild animals, he eats grasshoppers to live, and he sucks the juice from carob trees. And he teaches the people about virtue and goodness. And eventually Herod Antipas decides he should be imprisoned. He keeps him in prison for almost fifteen months, I think, and then one night his illegal wife's daughter Salome performs an erotic dance for the King and he is so pleased he offers her anything she wishes, even half the kingdom.

She asks her mother, "What should I ask for"?

She says, "Ask for John the Baptist's head on a silver plate."

Herod Antipas actually seems to be sort of getting along with John, but he keeps his promise and John's head is delivered to the daughter.

So Jesus is walking into a very dangerous man's home. Jesus himself has criticized Herod Antipas, called him an old fox. It's a very dangerous place to go: Herod is as paranoid as his father. He believes that John the Baptist's spirit has entered Jesus. He believes that Jesus has John's power inside him.

So Jesus is led through town, dragged by the Roman troops who are themselves extremely violent and frustrated, and they are afraid because of the masses of people in town who hate them. Everyone's uptight, nervous, tense. They drag him to Herod Antipas. Herod says, "I've heard about you a lot, I want you to perform some miracles for me. I heard you can do miracles. Let me see a few."

Jesus refuses to say a word. Herod tells his soldiers to beat Jesus. They beat him. He won't speak; he refuses to speak. Herod laughs, says, "You're a joke. You're not a powerful man. You're not a threat to me."

He doesn't even bother to kill Jesus. It would be like swatting a fly. He says, "Dress him in purple."

Purple is the color of the Roman emperor, Tiberius. Only one man in the whole Empire is allowed to wear that color. It comes from a rare seashell in the Mediterranean. But they find the purple cloth and they drape it around Jesus. They strip off his clothes. Jesus, the Great Messiah, the awaited prophet, the man who will liberate the Jews, the hope of every poor person in all of the four kingdoms, is standing there unable to do anything. People are punching him in the face. He's naked; he has a little purple cloth around his shoulders. Herod says send him back to Pilate, this man is a worthless joke.

They drag him back to Pilate. Pilate has been thinking. He knows Antipas might pull a trick like this, so he has another trick ready. The Roman Governor by tradition can release one important prisoner for the Passover holiday, and the Jewish people, the people of the city, get to choose which prisoner. There's a major prisoner that Pilate is holding and he wants to crucify him, but he's afraid of the reaction of the people. The prisoner's name is Barabas. He has murdered many people; he has lead a small uprising. He is considered a threat by the Romans, but they are afraid to kill him.

So Pilate has a good idea. He comes out to the crowd. The crowd is growing. The crowd is made now not just of the religious authorities but also of the people who cheered Jesus as he entered the gates Palm Sunday, who offered their donkey, who put the palm leaves on the ground.

There's a reaction starting to happen. Word is going around town. This man is a joke. This man is an impostor. This man is not holy. This man is not powerful. He is not what he claimed to be. The Romans dragged him to Herod's palace. Herod stripped him. Herod dragged him through the city with a little piece of cloth. He's not a miracle worker, he's not divine, he doesn't have power. The people are frustrated, the people are disappointed. They had great hopes, and like public opinion anywhere, suddenly it shifts one hundred and eighty degrees. They begin to hate this man who gave them so much hope, and who is obviously just a normal person.

And so when Pontius Pilate announces, "I will release to you a prisoner as by tradition—you can choose—but I allow you to choose Jesus. I know you love him." The people are angry. The people don't want this joke, this failure, this liar. They say, "Give us Barabas."

Pilate is amazed. He says, "No, I will give you Jesus. I agree I can do it."

They say, "We don't want him."

He says, "Well what do you want me to do with Jesus?"

They say, "Kill him. He's a joke. He's an impostor. He's not King David come back to us."

He's standing there naked, speechless—he can't even defend himself. If he can do miracles, why is he here?

Pontius Pilate has another problem; his wife has had many dreams about Jesus, the night before especially. She warned him: don't get involved, don't kill him, he's an extraordinary being. But Pilate is now backed into a corner. And I think he gets very angry at the situation. He says, "Bring me a bowl of water."

They bring a silver bowl of water, and he stands in front of the people, and he washes his hands and he says, " I don't have responsibility for this good man's blood. It's on your head."

They say, "We'll take it. He's a failure, he's an impostor, he's not a holy man."

And so I think now his brutal side comes out. He's in a position where he has to kill this man now. And he's angry that he has been put in the position. He hates the Jewish people.

So he says, "Okay, we'll do it your way," and he calls two of his men. He says, "Tie him [*sobbing*] to a stake." He says, "Get a scourge."

The people can't believe it. A scourge is a special whip. It has a long stick. It has leather straps: many. Each strap has metal and sharp pieces of bone tied into it.

He says "Scourge him." This is thirty-nine, by tradition, strokes of the scourge, whip. It's so difficult to whip a man with a scourge that two men have to take turns. It rips the flesh off of your body. Many prisoners die before they can get to the cross to be killed. And they whip Jesus with a scourge in front of the people. And at the end, Pilate is angry, he says, "Stand him up in front of the people."

The soldiers hold him up. He says, "Look what you got. Look, is this what you wanted?"

Pilate leaves. He tells the soldiers, "Take him in the cafeteria."

They have a large cafeteria for the soldiers in the fortress. He says, "Let the boys have some fun with him."

He's a joke; he's a loser. Everyone hates him: the Jews, and the Romans too. These soldiers are frightened, frustrated, bored between wars, like all soldiers. Now they have a authorized chance to really give it to a Jew.

So first they spit on him and beat him. He's already half dead. They then take a piece of red rope, put it around him, strip whatever clothes he had had. He's standing naked again, bleeding everywhere. And they make a crown, from some very terrible thorns, *jujup* thorns. They shove it on his head. They put a big oaken stick in his hand; they say, "Oh King," and they bow to him.

Then they take the stick and they beat him as hard as they can. The people are dismayed; the disciples are nowhere. Then they take him to be crucified. They put back on a single cloth around his waist.

The place of crucifixion is called Golgotha. It is west of the city gates on a hill.

It's almost three miles away. By tradition, the prisoner must carry his cross to the crucifixion. The upright part is dug into the ground. The cross part is the part that the prisoner carries. It weighs about 125 pounds; it's six feet long. They put it on Jesus' back.

There are large crowds of people lining the streets—thousands of Jews from all over the Mediterranean, Egypt, Greece, Turkey, Syria, Italy, Rome—they are all watching what's going on. This man is to be killed. He starts to drag the wood down the street; he collapses. The soldiers grab a Jew, from Egypt, I think. He doesn't know what's happening. They say, "You carry the top of the cross." And Jesus walks behind.

Jesus is losing it. He's ranting at the crowd. The women from Galilee are reaching out, crying to him. He looks back, he snarls at them, he says, "If you think this is bad, wait till you see what happens to the city."

And in their lifetimes, 90,000 Roman troops attack Jerusalem after a small uprising, and they tear it down, every single stone. Herod's temple, as big as, we said I think six football stadiums, is destroyed to the last rock. The Elders of the temple are dragged to Rome and killed. The treasure of the temple is offered to the emperor.

They reach the place of the crucifixion and they start to nail Jesus. It's large iron spikes. They don't put it through your hand; they put it through your wrist because there's a nerve there.

They nail him to the top piece. Then they raise it and then they nail your legs to the lower piece. There's a terrible addition to the cross. There's a small foot platform where you can stand your feet, which are already nailed. The prisoner will struggle to keep himself up with his feet, because if he relaxes he will suffocate.

In the Roman Senate, people like Cicero have even asked the emperor to ban crucifixion. It's just too cruel. A man will stand for twelve, fifteen hours, dying. Crows and other beasts will come and peck out his eyes.

So Jesus is put up with two people, two murderers, who are crucified next to him. They spit at him. These people are dying. They are as disappointed and angry as the other people in Jerusalem. "You said you would free us. You said you were divine. You said you had power. Look at you."

People stream out of the city. People stand around the cross to spit and yell insults. "You said you would help us. You said we could escape death itself. You said we would come to a kingdom. Look at you."

Jesus doesn't say anything. At some point, he cries out, "I thirst."

Somebody puts a sponge on a stick, pours vinegar on it. He can't drink it. And he's on the cross for six hours. He's thinking. He's dying of the pain and the loss of blood from the scourge. And no one comes to his aid. And then, just as evening comes, as the holy day, *Shabbat*, begins, he raises his head, and he cries to heaven.

In the Gospel of St John, John has cleaned up his last words: "Oh, I give my spirit to my Father."

Matthew has the real last words. In the earliest manuscripts, they are in Jesus' own language, Hebrew-Aramaic, and it says, *"E-li, E-li, lama sabact a-ni?"* [Crying.] "God, God, why did You forsake me?"

And in the last moment of his life, he loses his faith. He's a loser in every way. He has failed in every way.

And what about his disciples, the people he trained? There's Judas Iscariot, sold his teacher for the price of a shirt. There's a man who's been trained by his lama for all those years—he loses faith.

He can't believe what he's done. He goes to the religious authority. He says, "Take back the money, I did a wrong thing."

They say, "You keep it."
He throws it on the ground; they refuse to touch it. He goes and hangs himself.

What about the other disciples? What about the good ones? Peter, James, John, who went with him to the Garden of Gethsemane?

Oh, your teacher might be taken tonight to be killed, please keep watch. They fall asleep.

Jesus is concerned. He comes back, wakes them up, "Please, watch, it's dangerous tonight."

"Yes, yes, yes."

He goes back, to his prayers, they fall asleep again.

At the last supper, he serves them; he washes their feet. Imagine a holy lama like Khen Rinpoche coming to the door, taking off your shoes, and licking your feet as you enter. It's the same thing in their culture. No one says no; they just let him do it. Around the table at the last supper the night before, Jesus says, "They're going to take me, they're going to kill me. Here, every time you eat something, think of me. I'll be inside of you, my body. Every time you drink something, think of me. I'll be inside of you, my blood."

What is their answer? "Oh, Teacher, who among us will be the greatest after you leave?"

Jesus says, "I'm going to be killed; the man who is going to betray me is sitting at this table. He's the man who's dipping his bread into the soup right now."

They look. It's Judas. Judas says, "Is it me?"

Jesus says, "You have said it."

No one tries to stop Judas. No one tries to restrain him. He just walks out.

Peter says, "Don't worry Jesus. If they take you, they have to take me too."

Jesus turns to him, he says, "In this single night, before dawn, you will tell people three times you never heard of me."

Peter says, "Never, I will die with you. They will have to crucify me also."

After the mob comes from the religious authorities and takes Jesus, every disciple runs away. Peter is afraid, but he follows from a distance. At the house of the high priest he stays outside. He pretends to be just an innocent bystander. A woman comes to him and says, "I can swear I saw you with him in the temple."

Peter can see Jesus through the doorway. Jesus is being threatened and beaten. Peter says, "I never heard of him."

An hour later, another woman comes. "I can swear I saw you with him."

Peter says, "I swear I didn't know him."

She says, "You speak Galilean, your accent is Galilean. You must be one of his people."

He says "No, no, I never heard of him."

This is the man who Jesus has chosen to lead the church after his death. This is the cornerstone. His name is *Petra*, stone, for that reason. Jesus has given it to him. This is the most important disciple.

Another man comes, almost dawn now. He says, "I've seen you."

"Who are you?"

"I am the brother of Malcus."

"Who is Malcus?"

"Malcus is the servant of the high priest whose ear was cut off by a follower of Jesus last night. You look like the man…"

Peter says, "I swear to God, I never met this man."

Jesus turns from inside the room, he looks out at Peter, the rooster crows.

He collapses, he leaves, he hides, he cries. No one comes to the cross to help Jesus. His mother comes, like all mothers. The other disciples are afraid. They are hiding.

So the man is a failure. He couldn't be a bigger failure. He has even failed his own God, or his Father. He has lost faith in the last minute of his life. The disciples are dispersed, hiding. No one has come to help him. Everything has collapsed. All the hope is gone. All the teachings don't count for anything. And that's how it was on Friday, Saturday. The whole day today, and yesterday.

So today I thought be good to talk about failure. We've been talking about good deeds. We've been talking about sending your good karma to other people. But we have many more failures. We have many more mistakes. And we can use them. We can use our mistakes.

Holy Lama Khen Rinpoche, when he first gave the secret teachings in this country, that I know of, there was a small group of disciples. One woman raised her hand. She said, "Rinpoche, are you going to give us secret vows?"

Rinpoche said, "Yes."

She said, "I heard if you break those vows, you can go to the lowest hell."

Rinpoche said, "That's true."

And so she said, "Then why do you give us these vows? We can't keep them."

Rinpoche said, "That's true."

She said, "Then we'll go the lowest of the hells."

He said, "Well if you do, you can tell all the other people you're there because you broke your highest vows. 'I'm not like you other slobs here. I'm not here because I murdered someone or committed adultery or stole from people. I'm here because I broke my tantric vows.' And you can say it proudly."

Then he said, "Come on, when you fail in your spiritual practice, it's because you've been practicing."

The Kalmuk Mongolians have a saying—I don't remember it—*kudmush oogah* and *mohah oogah*, it's something like that. It means, "People who never do any work can't make any mistakes." We can't make mistakes in our practice if we're not practicing.

We are trying to be good people. And we are failing often. More times than we succeed. We try to practice the perfection of Patience, one of the highest bodhisattva commitments. I will tell you openly and honestly, I listened to the wonderful Asian Classics Institute tapes of this same book, *Bodhisattvacharyavatara*, The Guide to the Bodhisattva's Way of Life. Christie and I listen to them on Sundays.

I was inspired by this lama, this American lama, describing the perfection of patience so well. We turned off the tape recorder. We got up to prepare something like a meal. And I got upset and angry about some stupid small thing. And I thought, you just got through listening to two long hours of patience, spoken by yourself—so inspiring—and then you can't control your own heart in the next fifteen minutes.

I tell you honestly, I have gone to *sojong*—this is the holy ritual prayer for cleaning our bad karma—and I sit down in the among my other fellow retreatants, and I start to think of maybe a time that I got angry. And just thinking about it during the ceremony of purification, I get angry. You get angry purifying your anger. We're hopeless. *[Crying.]*

I'm not kidding. We say we're going to practice giving. We go to our yurt. Someone dear to us is in town for a few days; we dig through the junk that's been piling up. The best things we keep on the altar, because they're ours. We know that we will get to keep them if they're on the altar. And then the stuff we don't like so much goes in a bag of down on the side and then when a friend is in town you dig through the bag. We can't be generous. We have obstacles in our hearts. We can't give the things we really like.

Holy Lama and I watched the Pope on television one day, speaking at a large stadium near New York. And he said, "Don't give people your extras; don't give people the things you don't like. Give them what's dear to you, give them the major part of your income."

Rinpoche was amazed. He said, "Oh that's perfect."

We can't do it. We say we're going to respect other people's things, and then the first time we need something, we take. We live in country where no one needs anything much, we have everything. But the minute there's a shortage…I remember the gasoline shortages.

I was in India, I watched people fight over a half a gallon of kerosene for their stove. I said, "Americans never do that, we are more noble."

I came back during the oil crisis. People were shooting each other in the gasoline lines. We are generous as long as we have extra. We don't steal as long as we don't need. But the minute we need, all the ethics, all the Bodhisattva's code, goes out the window. We won't suffer for the sake of honoring our vows.

We're all like that. We say, "I'm going to practice the bodhisattva perfection of meditation. We sit down, maybe we don't even sit down. Maybe we figure out an excuse not to do it. We do that; the retreatants do that constantly. We have twenty-four hours a day to meditate. We're constantly trying to come up with new excuses not to. Then when you finally sit down, your mind wanders off, and you sit there for an hour, and you get up feeling great. You haven't thought about the subject once.

We go to prayers, holy higher secret prayers, together. We recite holy ancient texts, and all I can think about is the desserts after. We'll get to share Vajra Yogini's cake tonight. Wonder what kind the careladies have sent.

We do prayers together; everyone's wondering, "Did anyone notice I can do the Tibetan?"

We go to teach people, if they listen to us for a while we start feeling like a big shot. People start coming and treating us like a lama. Deep down inside, we like it; we get addicted to it. We start to criticize other teachers. We start to get angry if people don't come and bow to us, and give us some nice thing. It's our nature: admit it, we all have it.

We say we're going to do retreat in Arizona. In New York, we can't stop dreaming about the days in Arizona; in Arizona, we can't stop dreaming about the days in New York. It's true. We make so many mistakes, we fail at our practice, but there's a background, we are trying. We are really trying.

I used to work in the diamond company. I went to my holy—Yamantaka? No I don't think so, Chakrasamvara—boss, and he said, "You got that large order ready yet?"

It's Montgomery Ward's—30,000 diamonds. I said, "No, I don't."

He starts to look like he's going to have a heart attack. I said, "I can't get the stones."

This is like a mantra in the business for us, "I can't get the stones."

He says, "Did you try everybody?"

I say, "I tried everybody. There's a guy named Saritej Yogesh Madhvani—I'll never forget you—he's got the stones"

He says, "We'll buy em."

I said, "We can't agree on the price."

He says—I'll never forget it—he says, "How much does he want?"

"He wants two hundred and ninety-three dollars a carat."

"And so how much did you offer him?"

I said, "Of course I offered him two hundred and fifty. Then I went to two hundred and sixty. He won't move a dollar. I went to two hundred and seventy. I went to two hundred and eighty. This is humiliating for a buyer. You swore they weren't worth more than two hundred and fifty. I went to two hundred and ninety-two dollars and fifty cents. I'm not kidding. He's dragging me through the mud, but I have too much pride to go the extra fifty cents. That's why Montgomery Ward is not going to get their diamonds."
The boss pats me on the back. He says, "You're wonderful."

I'm amazed. I'm in awe. My jaw drops, "What do you mean? You're gonna lose this order."

He says, "You're brilliant." He says, "You found the market."

I said "What do you mean?"

He says, "When you get that close and you break a deal, you know what the thing is worth. If he won't take two hundred and fifty or sixty or seventy or eighty, or ninety, you know it's goddamn well worth two hundred and ninety-three."

I never thought of it.

He says, "You found the market. Diamonds don't cost anything, they're just stupid little rocks. If somebody wants them, they have value. If nobody wants them, they are worth nothing, and you found this invisible line called the market. You found the market. It's brilliant."

He taught me for years. He said, "Now, when you walk out of here, I want you to understand something. Every time we have a large order in the future, you break half the deals—you lose half the parcels of diamonds that come in. Then you know you're at the market. You know you're at the edge of the border where you can just barely buy the thing, and that's how we make money."

And so I think of my practice like that. When you are failing, you say, "There's one person in this group I really can't stand. I've tried, I've really tried. My patience breaks at this one person."

Then you should stay with them. You should keep them close to you. Then you know you're in the market. You see, when your patience is breaking half the time, and your patience is kept half the time, then you're right there in the market. You're right where you're supposed to be.

If you go to a retreat and you break down half the day, and you're crying and feel crazy, then you know you're in the market. When you have something to give someone and you're walking over to their yurt, and you can't decide whether you should turn back or not, you're in the market.

This is the market, and this is where we should stay. Our failures are a sign that we are on the edge, we are right at the edge of our envelope; we are stretching as far as we can. When you fail in your vows, when you fail in your holy bodhisattva activity, when you fail to be a good person because you are struggling to be a good person, you are in the market of being a good person. You don't have to worry about anything. You'll never go to a hell realm like that, because you are struggling to be good. The boss should pat you on the back. You're in the market, you're really in the market. People who never fail in their practice are not trying. People who never lose patience with other people are just avoiding the people who upset them.

So when you fail, carry your head proud. You have something to dedicate. I think it's a very holy practice to dedicate our failures, because we have failed in the line of duty. Other people fail who've never heard of bodhisattva activity. Other people fail who've never heard of vows. Other people commit bad deeds constantly, all day long, without the slightest hesitation. They never heard of the ten commandments, or they never heard of the ten non-virtues, and they could care less. So when you fail, be proud, you've failed because you are trying. People who don't try don't say, "I failed." And dedicate that trying.

There are three ways to dedicate it, like we said with the good karma. One is external. That one is trying to work with outside causes—things that have already happened; that one is like trying to work with cement that's already hard.

You meet someone you don't like, and you try to reason with them. The reason you're meeting a person you don't like is because you did the same thing to someone else before. It's too late to reason with them, you know that. You can talk to them, you can try to convince them that they are doing something wrong, but it's too late. If it works, be happy; if it fails, be happy. It was too late anyway. It's not under your control really. So bad things come to you, look at it like that. The result has already come out, the cement is already hard, it's too late really. Try. Try to make things better, but don't be surprised or upset if nothing works out.

You can also work at a level I like to think of as soft cement, or half-hardened cement. I like this practice; it's very similar to the *mo-mos* we talked about yesterday, the dumplings. Yesterday we said you can do a good karma, do a good project, work hard, and maybe it takes five, ten years. Then in the last hour, in the last day, give it away to someone else. Let them have the credit. Slip into the background, give it away right there, give it to others, let other people have it. It's a very powerful practice.

You can do the same with negative karmas. I worked in a truck company when was in college. I didn't have enough money to go to the college. I had some scholarship, but they required us to work if we didn't have enough money, and so I worked in a trucking company. We had to carry mostly big tents, like this one, around New Jersey and set them up for people. We had about seven or eight big trucks, and we learned to drive them. Often times you'd be on a work crew: the truck is an open truck, there are three guys on the crew, and there's only room in the front for two. And it's cold—New Jersey winter—it might be snowing. Someone has to sit in the back of the truck, in the open.

And there was this rule passed down, I don't know how many generations of students, but it was a beautiful rule: no one sits in the back alone. So one of the guys up front would get out of the warm truck and go sit in the back unnecessarily with the freezing guy. And this was a code of honor that we had.

In a big corporation, it's the same. We had a code of honor among the vice presidents; no one ever spoke it, we just knew. Generally in a large corporation there might be five or six vice presidents. We were board members, we could sit around the board of directors' table, and normally you are blaming each other for all the things, and competing with each other.

But when someone does something really bad, when someone makes a really serious mistake… I remember one person packed up a large parcel of diamonds and gold, very valuable, worth a considerable amount of the company's money, and sent it uninsured to the wrong address. And there's no way to prove it was ours. Actually it came back later, but at the time, this person would have almost ruined the company. And something strange happens in that boardroom; all the vice presidents they come around that person, and they protect them, and they support them—everyone—it's unbelievable. The boss says, "Who's fault was this?" and five people say, "Mine."

In the Monastery, we call it *kyiduk chikpa*. Just say the word, it's beautiful: *kyiduk chikpa*.

When you join the Monastery, they take you into a special room, up on the upper floors of the temple. You stand before the abbot and the monastery secretary. They take out a huge scroll. They say, "What's your college?"

I say, "Gyalrong."

Then they say, "What's your nationality?"

I said, "American, first American."

Then they say, "Are you accepted by the monks?"

"Yes."

"Then you can enter the *kyiduk chikpa*."

Kyi means happy, *duk* means sad. *Kyi* means things are going well. *Duk* means things are screwed up. *Chikpa* means one for and all for one. It means once your name goes on the scroll, then whatever good happens at Sera Mey Monastery, we all enjoy it together. And when a disaster happens, we all suffer together as one. We support each other in the good times, and we support each other in the bad times.

And they say, "Do you swear?"

And I say, "I swear."

And then they shake your hand and they say, "You're *kyiduk chikpa*, welcome to the family."

And so we have to share each others failures. This is the partly wet cement way. It could be anything. In our yurt, it happens like this. One of us picks up one of those Chinese thermoses *[laughter]*—it could be any thermos. It slips out of our hands, and these are made of a special glass, the inside sleeve, and it has this amazing quality like a cannon. It shoots very fine glass splinters around the whole yurt. And this is *kyiduk chikpa*. You have a choice, you can stand there and yell at the other person, or you can say, "We're *kyiduk chikpa*." And both people get down on their knees and spend a few hours cleaning up glass slivers.

This is a way in real life to share other people's problems and failures. When you see someone make a mistake, a big mistake, go to them and figure out a way to share the responsibility. Our natural tendency is the opposite—we want to divorce ourselves from this person's side as soon as they've made a big mistake. But when someone has done something really wrong, when there's been a real failure, then others of us in this group, others of us who are trying to practice together, we should stand with them. We should say it's our fault.

So look out for ways that you can help be *kyiduk chikpa*. Try to find ways to share other people's failures with them, and it's a very beautiful kind of dedication of karma.

I'll describe the inside wet cement version, and then we'll have refreshments.

This is *tong-len*, this is the *len* part of *tong-len*, taking other people's karma onto yourself. In the heart chakra, in the subtle energy center at your heart, there are countless mental seeds stored, ready to go off like tiny little crystals. They are not physical, they are not mental: they are energy, they are potential. And so the holy practice of *tong-len*, is—when you know someone else has made a bad karma, or looks to us like that, which is all we can ever say—then try to imagine that you could take away that karma from their heart.

Breathe in deeply. Imagine that the bad karma seed is coming out of their throat and their mouth, like a little evil black tiny spot. And then when you breathe in, imagine that it comes in through your nose, down your throat, into your heart chakra, and enters that infinitely tiny drop of primal consciousness. And then those of you who have learned this practice know you must destroy it in the moment that it enters the drop of your inner consciousness. There's a flash of light and the evil seed is destroyed forever.

You don't take the seed; you don't keep the seed. It never ripens for you or anyone. This is very important not to let it stay there, not even in your visualization, not even in your mental picture of it. As soon as it enters the edge of the sphere of the infinitely small drop of consciousness, you destroy it with a burst of white light.

So what's the good? Can you take other people's bad karma away?

No.

Prove it.

I'm here. I suffer. I don't know who else here is suffering. I am suffering. I suffered today already. If there is a being who could take away my bad karma, and if that being was compassionate, which they should be, I wouldn't have suffered today. It proves that karma cannot be taken away by other people. Or we wouldn't be here.

So why should I pretend I'm taking other people's bad karma away? When you work in the subtle drop of consciousness, you are manipulating simply by the focus of your own mind. When your mind focuses in that drop, it can actually move things around. It's the only way to move things there. It's the very act of focusing at your heart chakra, even if you have no idea what it's like, keep trying. Keep trying, over and over. It may take years before you really find it. That's okay. If you didn't try you wouldn't see it even after years.

And then you go inside, and you start—with your focus, with your concentration—to actually manipulate the karmic seeds there. And it's very important to understand that all the things you can see, all the things you even think are being projected from this drop. So if we can go into the drop, if we can manipulate the seeds there, everything in the world will change.

Are you saying I could stop a war on the other side of the world by fooling around with my inner drop of consciousness at my heart chakra?

Yes, that's what I am saying. It is happening in your world because of some violence you did.

That's the way to go to paradise. That's the way we get to heaven. It's much more powerful to work with wet cement. And so it's not a stupid exercise to imagine, as we dedicate out good karmas, to suck in other people's bad karmas. *Kyiduk chikpa*, we share your pain and happiness together; we are all one family now. And you suck in the bad karma, and you destroy it in your heart chakra. And this profoundly affects the future of the entire world. This profoundly affects the future of the entire world.

Ah whew, take a break. *[Laughs.]*

[Break]

So now we'll go to Master Shantideva's work, *The Guide for Bodhisattvas*. We all are trying to be bodhisattvas. And we get suggestions from him about where to send our good karmas, our good karmic seeds like little crystals from our hearts to other people's hearts. I changed the order of the verses to fit this teaching and frankly to fit the story of Jesus' crucifixion, but the numbers of the verses are there. Today our theme is failure, and Master Shantideva is going to send the good karma of writing his book to people who have failed in an ultimate way. Could you read the first verse?

Salim Lee:

**(4)   I don't know how many
Realms of hell there are
Hidden in our world;
But by this power may every person
Trapped in one instead find joy
In the joy of the Heaven of Joy.**

Master Shantideva begins to send his good karmic seeds out with the power of his own mind, to people in the hell realms. I have to try to convince you in the next few minutes that hell realms exist. It's not popular to speak of them. You are considered foolish by many people if you say you believe in the hell realms; other people will say you're just following the old books, and that's negative thinking. Other people just say, the world is wonderful, there can't be places like hell realms.

I keep thinking of the lady at my office in New York. One lady was pregnant and she was dealing with large amounts of topaz. We were very concerned for her health and the health of her child, because the color is imparted by radiation. The stones stay hot for different lengths of time, depending on the kind of radiation you use. But you have to try to imagine the danger of radiation: one tiny particle in a collision is freed from the substance, like a small piece of gem on your finger, and it easily cuts through your skin. It reaches a single cell in the first development of the child, and it goes inside the cell, penetrates the cell wall, and it hits part of the chromosomes, and it damages an infinitely tiny piece of the DNA chain in a single cell. All cancers start this way also. It's a single loose atomic particle, striking a single cell.

It's the same with karma, when the DNA chain is damaged, then the child will grow wrong, and you can imagine, in the time of two or three seconds in the womb, this DNA has been damaged, and then for thirty, forty, fifty, sixty, seventy years, this baby has a defect, a serious defect. So the idea that a tiny infinitely small damage in a seed can cause decades of pain—real pain—to the child and his family, her family. It's real; it's not a made-up thing. We know these things happen. The woman's child was damaged.

Karma is the same: a tiny imprint on that infinitely small dot of consciousness in your heart. These seeds are managed by thought alone. These seeds are planted, these seeds are moved around, these seeds' content is determined only by the focus of your own thoughts. And so if you do something very violent mentally, if your intention is very negative towards another person, then a seed is planted in your heart. DNA is damaged: karmic DNA is damaged. And then it matures like any seed, it takes time to grow. And then the seeds which are creating out reality, this tent, this desert, this sky, the earth you are sitting on, the thoughts you are having, all of that energy is coming from the tiny drop in your heart, and it's wearing out because it's happening.

Every time an hour goes by, the energy of thousands of good deeds you did in the past is finished. And when that energy is gone, we call it death. Try very, very hard, try hard to know: death is not an outside thing, it's a change in your consciousness. It's a change in your perceptions, that's all. The images being presented to your mind by the tiny karmic seeds wear out. And then you see something different. You see what the next seed in line offers to your mind. And if that seed is malignant, then you see a hell realm.

People try to look for hell realms, "Oh we'll dig a tunnel under the earth." It's not like that; it's a change in your perceptions. If you can watch a clock go from three to four o'clock, you can go from this realm to a hell realm. It's the same. You have to think about it a lot.

So Master Shantideva says first, "I send my good karma to people in the hell realms." In the hell realms, time slows down. You know when you are in pain, time slows down. And so the perception of time there is a long, long time. The karmic seeds don't allow your body to die. People say "What a silly idea. You mean you could have your head cut off and then get back up?"

Yes, it's a silly idea. Oh, where do you think your life came from? What's keeping this meat alive? Where does life itself come from? How can a small bag of guts and bones outlive a car or a house? How? Where does life come from? It's seeds, karmic seeds; they can do anything. It's not crazy to believe that you could be cut into pieces in a hell realm and then come back into another body, whole, and be cut up again, and again, and again. Because you're here, you're alive. Your body is as much as an impossibility as those bodies are.

Really read a modern physics book, Steven Hawking's great book, *Brief History of Time,* is classic, you should read it. One of the holy teachers made me read it; I didn't want to read it. But he's very honest at the end. He says, "We can't explain why things happen. There are contradictions which are impossible. Light itself moves like a particle sometimes and then moves like a wave sometimes. It almost acts as if it were two contradictory things at the same time."

We can't tell you even the position of a particle and tell you its speed at the same time. This is called uncertainty principle. It's a fancy way of saying, "We can't figure it out." Einstein himself introduced an idea called cosmological constant. It's a made-up fiction—and he admitted it—to explain things he couldn't explain. It's a big part of the theory of relativity. And it's frankly a fiction, and he said it's a fiction, but it has to be there or my idea is wrong. Modern physicists threw out the cosmological constant, and replaced it with their own fictions, and they—read his book, he's very frank—these are fictions, we don't understand.

How can life be produced? We don't know. The forces which exist in balance to create human life are beyond possibility. The very energy of an electron in relation to the other particles, if it were a millionth of a percentage different life would be impossible. We can't explain why it came out like that.

So hell realms exist. I could give you the historical argument. Oh, Christians also say that. The Jewish scriptures also say that, and the Muslim scriptures also say that. Dante's description and Arya Nagarjuna's description are the same. But I think if you are an intelligent person, it's more powerful to explain the real cause of hell, which is the seeds in our own minds.

Then Master Shantideva says, "May their seeds be changed, may the hell realms become the Heaven of Bliss." This is a Buddha Paradise. Enlightened realm. He sends his good karmas to them for that. Next verse.

Pearl Steel:
(5) **May those who freeze in the cold of hell**
    Be covered in warmth.
    May infinite showers of gentle rain
    Fall from vast bodhisattva clouds
    To cool the searing pain

Of those who live there in fire.

[Laughing.] Thank you. Nice job.

I'll tell you some tantric secrets, what the heck. *[Laughs.]* We have three principal subtle channels in our bodies, the two smaller ones on the two sides and a larger one in the middle, running roughly down the area of the backbone.

All of your experiences of something hot, of motion, are ultimately triggered from the channel on the right side. Your perception of a sun is being emanated by the energy of the channel on the right side. Those of you who have studied emptiness deeply, you know. It's the idea of grasping to things as self-existent, the idea that things come from their own side and not from us. Every time you think that in a certain way, then that energy on the right side is moving in a certain malignant way, a wrong way. And ultimately that has created all our perceptions of moving objects and the sun itself, the heat within our bodies.

On the left side, the other half, are ignorant ideas about the nature of our own minds, triggering forces which have created objects like the moon itself. Your perception of the moon is an image presented to your mind through the influence of this channel, due to mistakes in the past.

If these subtle energies are disturbed in a serious manner, by serious negative wishes towards your fellow man, then those same energies create two forms of hell realms. One is the hells which are extremely hot. They are huge, dark caverns filled with screaming people running across an iron ground which is red-hot. There's nowhere to go, they just run and scream. You can't find them; no one made them. Do you think Lord Buddha was a fool? Do you think he thought some construction company went underground and built these places? They are being produced by your own mind, and they are real therefore.

In the upper caverns, people just sit in snow and ice, and scream and whimper in pain. So Master Shantideva is sending his good karma—may the people in the cold hells be blanketed in a sweet warmth; may the people in the hot hells, may this beautiful rain descend on them. From where? From bodhisattva clouds. What's a bodhisattva cloud? It's the simple action of taking care of other people. It's the simple action of destroying the ignorant selfishness that ruins our lives. Next verse.

Susan Stumpf:
(6) May the forest of falling leaves of knives
Turn for those who live there into
A pleasure grove of shady bowers.
May the daggers of the trunks
Of the trees of Shalmali
Sprout as the Wish-Giving Tree instead.

Surrounding the caverns of hell there are other hells, like concentric circles. People in the hot hells, they see at a distance trees, and they believe that they can run there and find some comfort. They run under the trees, and then the leaves become one like large knives, like razors, and they drop down and they cut the people's bodies, cut off little chunks. It is a creation of former very evil negative thoughts about others. People came to you for protection and you failed them, you refused them.

I want to be clear that if you are really trying and you fail to give help and protection to others you don't have to worry. The malignant seed won't be perfect. This seed can only come if you give up the wish to help. This seed can only happen if you fail and you don't care that you failed. Those of us who fail and go home and feel bad, you don't have to worry. The pureness, the purity of your sadness will clean that karma.

So really we just have to keep wishing we could protect others, and try as hard as we can, and not refuse anyone up to our capacity. Then we fail, and we know we're in the market.

There's a tree in the hells called Shalmali. Shalmali means a kind of a dagger. If you've ever seen palm trees up close, they have these sharp daggers of wood, pointing up near the top. People are being chased across the hell realm's floor by wild beasts, like large German shepherds. They have iron teeth. They are ripping the people's legs open. They see a tree, they try to climb it, and the branches which are like swords, turn downwards, and they cut the people open. You have a choice of climbing up against the swords or dropping to the dogs. When you get to the top and the dogs go away, you want to climb down—the swords reverse. This means the karma of a promise to help someone, giving them hope, and then changing. Someone comes to you for hope, for help, and instead you take advantage of them.

Again, this seed can't be planted for this hell if you are struggling to be good. We are all trying, struggling to be good. People here, all of us who sit at nights in our yurts and wonder why we can't be better people, just the wondering, just the wishing we could be better, changes the karmic seeds of failing others. And they will produce a sweet result.

Next verse.

David Stumpf:
(7)   **May the caverns of hell suddenly echo forth**
        With the soft sweet song of the dove and nightingale,
        Ruby-throated sparrow, graceful swans, birds
        Of every kind, drawn to the gentle waters
        That spring up instantly there, covered with lotuses
        Whose delicate fragrance fills the air.

Perhaps the worst thing in the hell realms is the sound of millions of people screaming. And the poetry is very powerful. The idea that suddenly the screaming stops and people are listening, and suddenly they hear these beautiful songs of birds. Every kind of sweet song of a bird that you can imagine. And some of them are the songs of birds which are only attracted to lakes and ponds. And then suddenly, in the middle of the fire, a pond appears and beautiful trees, and birds are landing in huge flocks and singing beautiful songs, and the fires are receding and beautiful huge lotuses are growing out of the cool water.

Master Shantideva is manipulating mental images in his own heart chakra to try to actually change the reality of hell. It's a very powerful action. More powerful than anything any of us can do externally. Next verse:

Eugenie:
(8)   **May the heaps of burning embers of fire become piles**
        Of precious jewels, and the red-hot glowing iron floor
        The ground of a new world, sparkling in crystal light.
        May the mountains that slam together, crushing the crowds
        Of helpless people between them, turn to the palace
        Temples of heaven, filled with bliss-filled Buddhas.

So Master Shantideva is going into his own heart chakra, he is entering his own drop of consciousness, he is manipulating infinitely tiny karmic seeds by focus itself, by the act of focus itself. And he is imagining that the embers and the hot coals in hell turn to jewels. There are special mountains in the hells: people are herded in huge masses between the mountains. And then the mountains slam together and crush them. The mountains open again, the people rise again, the mountains crush them again.

I think many of our very basic phobias, like afraid to be in a small place, or afraid to be in a high place; I think they are vestiges of our formal hell lives. We have basic instinctual fears, even of death, which I believe are driven by a deep unconscious knowledge of what can happen after. And so he's praying that these huge mountains should turn into beautiful crystal palaces, and inside there are just Buddhas singing, and hell becomes a paradise.

The very act of imagining it changes seeds in your heart chakra. The world begins to change itself. It's an incredibly powerful way of helping others. Next verse.

Tara Melwani:
(9) In the moment that I speak may the great rain of putrid
 Filth, and stones of solid fire, knives, and spears,
 Transform into a soft steady shower of fragrant flower petals.
 And in the hells of anger, where people snatch up rocks
 And sticks to gash one another open, may they instead
 Gather up armfuls of petals, laughing, tossing over each other.

There's a special part of hell: it's one of the easier parts of hell. When you're born there, you just assume a body like, maybe like ours. And the minute you open your eyes, there's someone running at you with a stick or a rock, and they are trying to beat your brains out. And due to your karmic seeds, you are filled with anger. You search, you try to find any kind of a sick or a stone, and you pick it up and you fight back. And you can imagine a vast plain, burning plain, dark, huge groups of people just trying to bash each other's brains out with rocks, all day, all night, no rest, no stop. When someone dies, they just get up again.
That's impossible!

Your life is impossible. It comes from anger and violence and competitive thoughts towards each other. Why are vows eight and nine of the ten non-virtues, why did they make it into the top ten? Out of eighty-four thousand. Number eight is being unhappy that other people have gotten something nice. Number nine is being happy that trouble has come to other people. We must be having some version of these thoughts about a thousand times a day if it's in the top ten. And if you truly examine your heart, you will find those thoughts there, even at this moment.

And so in a way we are already picking up rocks and trying to smash each other's heads. But just the intention, just the wish that other people should have problems, which I openly confess I have all the time, creates a malignant seed and it ripens into this hell realm.

You fight it: how? With your book, with your diary, with watching your vows and your own heart from hour to hour. It doesn't take much, just write down the truth. "I had a thought about this other person I was envious of. I was hoping they would have a little trouble."

The very act of focusing on the true condition of your own heart with honesty ruins that nice evil seed, and makes it into a beautiful seed. Do your diaries. It doesn't change us overnight. You don't have to be a hundred percent sincere. You can be tired and scribble down something half true. But the very act of looking at your own heart, the very act of going into your mind and admitting that we don't wish well on others, ruins that nice hell seed, and it becomes the seed for a bodhisattva. Next.

Bonnie Moore:

(10) I send the awesome power of the good deed that I've done
As well to all those trapped within the river that cannot
Be crossed, wrapped within the hell-flame there, with all
The skin and flesh ripped away from their bodies, the bones
Jutting out in the glistening white of freshly fallen snow;
May this power grow their bodies back, in the form of
divine Angels.

One of the last of the surrounding hells is a special kind of river. It doesn't flow with water, it flows with fire. Inside the flowing fire are small creatures. The closest thing in this realm is like a piranha. People are running to escape from the dogs, the very evil birds that peck at them, the special beings, guards at the hells who are trying to cut them open. And they run into this river. They can't ever reach the other side. No one ever reaches the other side. Every time they put their foot down, the fire and the creatures rip the flesh away. When they raise their leg, the bones are jutting out, and in the time it takes to lower their leg again, the skin has grown back. Master Shantideva says, when their leg comes up, may they turn into a Tantric deity, and fly away. He is praying for that.

I think this is a statement on how we treat others who are on the very end of their rope, people come to us for help. As a bodhisattva, we have a special responsibility when another person has nowhere else to go. If you have knowledge that a person has another option, if you know that a person has someone else to turn to, then your bodhisattva vows allow you to refer them, direct them, to another person. But if you honestly know that this person has come to the end of their hope, if you're honestly aware that this person has nowhere, if you know that everyone else in the world would reject them—waste of time, hopeless, too much trouble, incredible trouble, maybe even crazy—then you have to take them in, we have to take care of them especially. They have reached the river at the end of the hells.

We don't always succeed, you know, I know. People have come for our help, they have been maybe difficult people, people with major problems. And we have tried to help them. Maybe not as much as we could, but we really tried. And it failed in the end. But if you truly wanted to help, if you truly tried to help to your capacity—our capacity is not very big, we're not perfect—but make a special effort to help people who are beyond help, and you will never have these seeds. We can fail gracefully.

I'd like to take a break there and we'll finish shortly.

Now I listen to old tapes from New York. He always says, "We're about done," and I know dinner is an hour away. Okay, we'll take a break.

[Break]

Next verse please.

Michael Moore:

(11)   And then may the beings in hell take pause,
            and wonder suddenly to themselves,
            "Why now do the henchmen
    Of the Lord of Death, and his vicious
            ravens, and the birds of prey,
            Why do they turn and run from us?"
    What glorious power has turned the night of hell
            to golden day, and smothered us within
            this happiness, this strength, this bliss?
    Who could have such power?" And may they raise
            their eyes and see the blue
            of sky, and seated in it
    The One Who Holds the Diamond in His Hand.
            And then may joy spread
            in their hearts, so powerful that
    It tears away every wrong they ever did,
            and so then they can rise
            and fly—fly away with him.

It's a very beautiful image. People in this huge cavern of darkness are screaming, running from hell guards. They were not hired by some employment agency. They are a projection of the same evil malignant karmic seed in your own heart chakra, like every irritating person you've ever met. And suddenly the guards are running the other way and suddenly all the vicious animals like Nazi German shepherds are running the other way. Suddenly the darkness in the hell turns into this glorious sunlight. Suddenly the dark cavern roof turns into a beautiful blue sky. And the people are amazed. They don't know what's happening.

They look up in the sky and there seated on a sun is a bodhisattva. In Sanskrit, his name is *Vajradhara*. Also called *Vajrapani*. And he has driven away the hell guards and the evil animals and the darkness. And they are so happy, they have such joy that it pierces the heart chakra, it pierces the subtle drop of consciousness, it goes to the center of the karmic seed and explodes it, and they are finished with their hell life. There won't be any more hell life. There is no more hell, and they just fly away with him.

all other Jesuses. The fact that no other Jesus exists or no other Buddha exists, or no other us exists. It's not that we don't exist—that's not emptiness. It's not that we don't have a body—that's not emptiness. It's that if you took away the Michael Roach that I am—that my karmic seeds are creating right now, you wouldn't have any other. If we took away the speaker today that you are seeing, who is created by your karmas, there wouldn't be anything else.

There is no base reality. There is no way that things are and you are looking at it. There isn't even any way that things are and you are interpreting it. Everything is your interpretation. There is no way that I am, or any other person is, or you are. Everything is being driven by your karmic seeds. All things are a perception. Which is why we can go from hell into paradise—it becomes a simple matter of collecting the right seeds carefully, persistently—it takes time. And then when you get a good karmic seed, well you goddamn well better think about it and give it away.

Put it clearly in your mind: "Today I went to that teaching. I sat there for god knows how many hours, and I really tried to listen. I'm not perfect, I was bored sometimes, I wandered sometimes, my ass hurt sometimes, but I tried hard. I got a good karmic seed in my mind."

That's called crystallizing the seed. The focus on it crystallizes it. Then you have to send it to someone. You have to give it away to someone. I send it to one of my holy teachers that I doubted or I was disrespectful to this afternoon. *[Laughs.]* I'm not talking about me. I'm talking about a seed that I have that I would like to send to myself. And we can all do that. That's why emptiness is our savior. We exist, all these practices—from the first day you ever heard of Buddhism to the final days of your Tantric practices in some yurt somewhere—they all relate to trying to see ultimate reality.

On that day, those fifteen minutes, you will clearly and directly see the enlightened awakened being that you are to become. And it will be unstoppable. At that moment you will see directly into the future. You will see—oh what the heck, seven lifetimes—it's nothing. And then you will be the holy, sweet, enlightened one who helps countless people on this world and other worlds. You will see this if you haven't already, and this is why we are here. This is the only reason we are here.

And so Master Shantideva's Bodhisattva Manjushri, the angel of emptiness is

>   that you have come to us,
>   and smashed the terrors here?
> Are you not the one
>   to whom a thousand gods
>   would run, to touch
> The tips of their crowns
>   at your lotus feet?
>   The one whose eyes glisten
> In tears of compassion for us?
>   The one on whom
>   A constant shower of petals falls?
> See him now—surrounded by palaces
>   filled with crowds of celestial maidens
>   singing out his praises!"

The next great Bodhisattva comes, the third one. It is Gentle Voice: in Sanskrit, *Manjushri* or *Manjughosha*; in Tibetan, *Jampel Yang* or *Jampeyang*. He represents the Buddhas' knowledge; he represents the understanding of emptiness. So already we've had the Bodhisattva of the Secret Ways, then the Bodhisattva of Kindness, and now Master Shantideva devotes to verses to the Bodhisattva of the Knowledge of Emptiness.

Emptiness is the key to everything. The reason we even have retreat centers, the reason there are any classes at all, the reason people are working so hard to teach, the reason people are in retreat, the reason you are doing retreats, the reason holy Lama Khen Rinpoche ever came to this country was to try so hard to get each person here to see emptiness directly. It takes fifteen, twenty minutes. It takes years of effort and preparation.

All the secret methods as well, all the exercises with which we try to affect our inner channels: breathing exercises, physical postures, everything, all the special meditations are directed towards causing, triggering with in the deep channels, the direct perception of emptiness. Again, emptiness is not some void or nothingness. It's an extremely powerful reality above our reality. And you can intellectually understand it as the fact that Jesus or any other person around us is only what we perceive and nothing else.

At some point you are able in deep meditation to perceive directly the absence of them. Bask in the glow of the holy words of Master Shantideva, the story of Easter, and just try to imagine what they would like. Try to pass them the food they would enjoy. Try to talk about the thing they would enjoy talking about. Try to put yourself across the table in their body, and simply try to take care of them first, as if they were you.

This extinguishes the fire of all pain and unhappiness. It's so easy. All of us are at times unhappy. We are all at times confused. We are all nervous about our lives. We are all concerned that we aren't Buddhas yet. But the solution is so easy: just think about other people. Just try to make other people happy. Next verse.

Ven. Lobsang Chunzom:
(13) **And then may the hell beings**
>> **hear a voice that**
>> **calls to them and says:**
> **"Come my friends, so far away,**
>> **cast away your fears now,**
>> **and come be at my side;**
> **Come to the one whose power**
>> **has stripped away your agony**
>> **and thrown you into joy."**
> **And when they lay their eyes on this one,**
>> **on Gentle Voice himself,**
>> **may every miserable creature there**
> **Burst forth in a song, a song**
>> **that roars throughout the hells,**
>> **a song that sings:**
> **"You are the bodhisattva who protects**
>> **every single living being,**
>> **overcome by your love for them;**

I think we have to read the next verse too.

Debbie Bye:
(14) **"You are the youth divine,**
>> **with your flowing locks,**
>> **body blazing in light;**
> **How could it be**

not a great moral teacher. He's not an idiot or a fool, or incompetent, or a failure. He's only what thou sayest. He's only what you see. That's his emptiness. It's no big deal. Karma operates in your heart chakra. The *vasanas,* the subtle seeds, ripen. You perceive this historical being as something good or bad or indifferent or whatever your karmic seeds force you to see. It's not a choice. Even if you change your mind this weekend about Jesus, it's because your own seeds have changed. That's the emptiness and karma relating to one person.

And Vajrapani holds a diamond bolt in his hand to represent that. It's a beautiful fact that the shape of the *vajra* is the shape of a twinned diamond crystal. All diamond crystals which form under perfect conditions, form themselves into the shape of the *vajra* that we use in our special prayers. And all of you have studied the diamond cutter and you know what it represents. Next verse.

Cathy Hinman:
(12) May a rain of lovely flower petals
    mixed with cool and perfumed water
Descend in a song and extinguish the flames
    of the fires that burn in hell.
May the beings who live there look upon
    this sight, and suddenly
Be overcome by happiness. And then
    may they think to themselves,
"Who could have done this thing?"
    And may they turn and see
Before them the One who holds
    the Lotus in His Hand.

A second of the eight great bodhisattvas appears in the sky, sends down a gentle rain of flowers and extinguishes the hell realm fires. This is "the one who holds the lotus in his hand," the name for *Avaloketeshvara,* or *Chenrezig.* You can say Dalai Lama.

It's not a big mystery. What can change misery into happiness? What can make each of us here, and what can make me happy? What can make you happy is just taking care of other people. Sit with someone this evening. Have a meal with

And so, I ask you again, there's almost a little more than a year left. The retreat actually goes three years and three months. You have about a year left. I ask you again from my heart, I beg you, finish the courses, finish the eighteen courses of the open teachings. Get yourself ready, please. It's not difficult. We sit and drink hot chocolate and listen to the stupid guy ramble on. Then you fill out a few questions, and that's all. You can easily do it. But if you haven't had time up to now, you have to turn on the gas now. You'll run out of time. The time will come and you won't be ready, and it doesn't work. Even with the best intentions of a teacher, if the student is not ready, it actually causes trouble to try to lead them into the secret teachings.

Along with the courses, you have to try to develop your hearts. *Vajrapani*, which means the one who holds a *vajra*. *Vajra* has been called thunderbolt or diamond bolt, because in the old days, when lighting struck a rock or a tree, it split it—it burst it apart. We had one here, close by. It was extraordinary. It was a huge oak tree under which we all used to sit for classes when we began retreat. And one night, lighting struck it and just broke it in two. And in the old days, people thought if lighting could do that, it must have a diamond at the very tip of it, because they knew that nothing could scratch a diamond. But the diamond in Vajrapani's hand—and his name means "diamond in my hand"—represents the two great concepts of the open teachings: emptiness and karma.

No one here, I'm sure, would ever have a mistaken idea about emptiness by now. It's just the emptiness—you can say the emptiness of Jesus, for example. Some people saw him as a savior, as a messiah; some people saw him as a competitor—even when he brought people back from the dead. Some people saw him as a political threat. Some people saw him as an idiot, a fool. The people in Jerusalem at the end saw him as a failure, an incompetent impostor. Everything he claimed about the eternal realms, and eternal life, and kingdoms of heaven—was obviously a lie, since he is up there on this cross bleeding to death.

Even nowadays, all of us, we come from different backgrounds. We can have different perceptions of historical Jesus. Some people mildly respect him. Some people have a very bad experience about maybe some church they went to as a child, and they equate it with ties that were uncomfortable, or long boring talks.

That's the emptiness of Jesus, nothing more mystical than that. He doesn't have a nature; he's not a divine being. He's not a human in contact with the divine. He's

It sounds a lot like some kind of a god who can just drop down into hell when he feels like it and bring everybody out. If he was a real god, and if he cared for those beings, there wouldn't be any hell realm. They would've left before it began. There is no such being, and the existence of our own suffering proves it. We have to take responsibility for our own world and our own lives. We created them, we are experiencing them, and only we can stop them. No one can change your karma for you. No one can take your karma away from you. The fact that we suffered this afternoon—I did—proves that they can't if they are compassionate.

So what is Master Shantideva describing? Here begins a section about the great— they're called *nyeway sey gye* in Tibetan—eight great bodhisattvas who are particularly close to Lord Buddha. Each one comes to the hell realms. We will see four of them. And they change the hell realms.

How can an outside person change my world? I have to do it myself. I have to clean my malignant karmic seeds. I have to do such pure deeds that I produce a new world.

Master Shantideva is talking about the secret identities of these bodhisattvas. Vajrapani is in truth a tantric deity, and he represents the entire secret teachings. I think when I say secret or tantric, old seeds come up in your mind and you think of cults in dark little caves, and maybe a few candles, and a skull full of blood maybe. But actually the secret teachings are these beautiful crystal mansions of golden light, whose foundation is purity in your ethical life—purity towards all, compassionate kindness towards all beings. The secret teachings are founded on these ideas. They are the extension of these ideas. They are the natural outcome of being kind to countless people. They are full of light and purity.

And so Master Shantideva is saying if you want to really change the hell realms, if you care that people that you can't see might be suffering, tormented—unspeakably—then try to enter the secret teachings. Find a qualified teacher of those secret ways, educate yourself properly, get yourself prepared out of love for all beings who might be in pain.

It's my hope that the sweet secret teachings could be imparted to many kind and holy people through all of our work. But from your side, you must prepare. It's foolish, and frankly it can lead to great sadness and problems if someone tries to show you the secret ways, and you're not already prepared.

changing the hell realms into paradise. Next verse.

Dorathea Spaeda:
(15) **Oh thus may it come to pass,**
    through the power of the goodness
    that I've done:
Every suffering being in hell,
    wrapped now deep in happiness,
    standing staring up
At clouds as they gather overhead,
    and the reality
    of the bodhisattvas—
The one whose name is
    Sheer Excellence,
    and all the rest—
Uncovered fully in the light,
    sending down upon them
    showers of the rain
That brings them bliss,
    cool soft rain,
    rain of finest fragrance.

Thank you. Sheer Excellence is the name of one of the other eight great Bodhisattvas. In Sanskrit it's called *Samantabhadra*. In Tibetan, *Kunsang*. This Bodhisattva is known for Samatabhadra's offerings. It's a beautiful offering. You imagine the whole sky covered with sweet roses. I like roses in the sky—it could be any flower you like. But these beautiful flowers and holy offerings to the enlightened ones and all suffering beings spread throughout the entire daytime sky, like flowers floating every few feet from each other, all the way up to the end of the atmosphere. And you imagine them and you give them. Master Shantideva has asked the Bodhisattva of Giving to come.

Those of you who studied this scripture know that its structure is based on the six perfections. And that oddly the first perfection, giving, isn't covered in the entire book in a separate chapter. And here Master Shantideva reveals that this is the chapter on giving. It's the chapter on the ultimate way of giving. Not to work with outside objects, which is so primitive and so limited. How many coffees can you make for people? How many small gifts can you give to others? It's very limited.

How much protection can you really give to all the people in New York today who were beaten, or robbed, or raped?

You can't work with dry cement very well. We have to try. It's our obligation; it's our honor. It's a commitment we've made to protect others and give to others what we have. But ultimately, we must work at the level of causes. We must learn to enter the chakra of consciousness. We must learn to enter the storehouse of karmic seeds; we must learn to fix the DNA, and then teach others to do it. And that's the real giving. That's giving at an ultimate level. Next verse.

Ramon Alonzo:
(16)   And by this power may every being
        Who lives in the animal realm be freed
        From the terror of feeding off each other.
        May those who live as craving spirits
        Enjoy a life of peace and plenty,
        Like humans of the isle of Haunting Voice.

We're on the next to the last verse. Master Shantideva has concluded his gift of his good karmic seeds to the beings in the hell realms. Now he goes to the beings in the animal realm—the first half of this verse. I grew up in cities like you, most of you probably. I didn't have much contact with animals except with pets—dogs or cats or things like that. But here, something different has happened. I think it's very joyful. I'd like to tell you about it. It's very exciting for us who are in retreat. We are city folk really, and it's always a joy to see these things happen.

I think because we are quiet—we don't speak normally except when you're here. And, because we are trying so hard to keep our minds in meditation and good thoughts, we don't have other obvious distractions to prevent us from trying to keep our minds in a holy place all day. And I think because of the quietness of our minds, and the quietness of our voices, then slowly, slowly, very slowly over the two years, the animals have come to us. Very, very gradually. At first, it was the dumb ones, like lizards, and the—OK, not so dumb ones. But now it's really exciting.

This afternoon is an example—we were sitting there, we were reading a book, and a rabbit came to the door, the screen door, and he actually banged his shoulder on it. And he wants a cookie. And we open the door and he hops inside. If you see a wild rabbit in the wild, you will only get a quick glimpse, because they run. But they are, they treat us as family now. It's very beautiful. We have other animals that come. Even coyotes come. It took a long time for the coyotes, and they don't eat from our hands yet, but almost. They will come inside the fence and eat close by us, and they are very beautiful.

But there's something very sad. There's really something sad. I came to realize that I can't love them too much. I came to realize I can't get too attached to them because they constantly are killed. You see a baby rabbit, a few inches long. You befriend him slowly over a year or two, and then you walk out one day, and his body is there, and his chest is torn out. And you learn that it's very hard emotionally for a person who's in retreat all day, and befriends another creature, to see them murdered, or lying on the ground. It's almost like your mother was killed. We don't have other friendships, or people around us, so we become very attached to the animals. But they are constantly being killed by each other.

I know that many animals are special. There are many stories—true stories—of amazing kindness from animals to other animals. But if you live here and you watch the animal realm, it's a terrifying place to be. Each smaller animal lives in terror of the larger animal. There's a food chain. The animals are extremely alert constantly. You can't make the slightest move, you can't make the slightest sound. They'll be a hundred yards away if you sneeze or cough while you're feeding them. Because they depend on their wits and their speed for survival. Because they all eat each other; they all live off killing each other. Most of them. And so they are very, very hesitant to even approach us for months and months because they are so afraid. And afraid of each other.

So Master Shantideva is sending his good karma, his good karmic seeds. I pray that all those beings in the animal realm may be freed from this violence which is done to them. And, it's important to say that humans are a big part of the food chain. We are always killing animals, either purposely or by accident. Often just simply by neglect. We don't stop to think that we use the skins of the animals, or we take advantage of their trust in us. He's praying that we should all be freed from this kind of violence.

I'd like to read the last verse because it connects to the second half of this verse.

Maia Farrell:

**(17) May a stream of milk descend from the hand
Of the Lord of Power, the Realized One,
The One Who Looks with Loving Eyes,
And may it fill the spirits who crave,
Washing them too in a gentle bath,
Leaving them cool and refreshed.**

There's another realm we can't see. There have been reports in western culture. People call them ghosts. People say a house is haunted by ghosts. We have stories of poltergeists. We have stories of wraiths or other kinds of spirits, especially around houses, things like that. Buddhism teaches that there is a kind of realm of spirits. These are beings who, when they were human, were overly attached to objects. It could be attachment to your house, it could be attachment to physical objects like the things you own. It is a malignant seeds' result—the malignant seed was trying to grasp onto physical objects—trying to own them, trying to collect them, piling them up in your home, always trying to get the best ones for yourself, always giving the lousy ones to others. And over a lifetime these small seeds pile up, and as you die, you feel intense attachment and pain that you are going to lose these physical objects which you have collected.

Every object you leave in your house is a danger. Every object you allow to be in your house is a danger. During your life it takes up a certain part of your mind. If you have too many of those objects, you will never be able to meditate, because of course a part of your mind has to catalog, has to be aware, where is that object now? Where is my favorite rosary? Where is my favorite Buddha image? Where are those nice things that people gave me? And you remember. If you remember where they are, it means they took part of your mind. Those objects stole part of your thoughts, your mind. Part of your memory is occupied. Part of your attention is not available to give to your meditation.

These objects are deadly enemies of Buddhist practitioners. This is a no-brainer—you have to get rid of them. Really, give them to the Goodwill. Give them away to people who are not trying to meditate. And every object you leave in your home, as you die, there's a grave danger. I'm not being poetic. This is serious. This is like having a big ball of radiation in your house, or poison in your water. It can kill you. It can take you to a *preta* realm. If in your last few moments of your life you reflect sadly on some idiotic physical object that you own, it can take you to a bad realm. So it's wiser now to get rid of them.

Master Shantideva is praying for the beings who have gone to this realm. They often stay around the thing they were attached to. Their bodies are made of very subtle physical matter—we can see them only under special circumstances. The things people call ghosts are like them, but they are counted in the millions. There are thousands on this land that we are sitting on. They wander hopelessly, attached to idiotic physical things they owned or they lived under, and they suffer. They have a special karma that due to their selfishness and possessiveness they can't enjoy anything. You can see this karma growing in people before they die, people who have put their trust and hope in physical objects are, as they approach death, very sad. They suffer a lot. They try to cling to those objects. And so Master Shantideva is trying to send help—the karmic seed of his good deed—to the people who are suffering intensely from the disease of possessiveness.

We'll see you tomorrow, and thank you for coming. We get all excited when you're here. We talk sign language about who we saw under the blindfold, and it makes us really, really happy that you are here. It's a very bright time in our lives. Thank you.

Fourth Day:
Easter Sunday, March 31, 2002

We'll meditate for a few minutes. Okay, we'll start.

Then after Jesus had passed on the cross it was becoming late. It was getting dark and the holy day was about to begin. There was a custom if the people were crucified that if they didn't die quickly enough, in this case the execution must be finished before the holy days begin, and so it was a custom to take a strong club and break the prisoner's legs under the knee. Then they couldn't hold themselves up anymore on the little footpad and they would suffocate.

Jesus has already passed. The Roman soldiers are supposed to check. One of them holds a spear and reaches up and jabs it into his side and he bleeds, but he's dead. They decide not to break his legs, but they break the legs of the two murderers at his side. Then a man named Joseph from another country, a Jew exiled, one of the many of the diaspora—he is wealthy, he has been a secret follower of Jesus—and he goes to Pontius Pilate and asks if he could have the body of Jesus.

I think we can assume a large bribe was paid to the Roman governor—this was common in those days—and Pilate agrees. Joseph has already prepared a tomb for himself. It's really just hole dug out of stone in the side of a hill near a garden or a grove, and inside it's quite small, maybe four, five feet long and about three, four feet wide, and there's a simple stone slab on which to place a body. And Joseph the wealthy man says, "Please put him in my tomb," and the *Shabbat* holy day is coming on.

They wrap Jesus' body in linen cloth, which is the custom, and then they put him in the tomb, and a large boulder, a slab of rock, is placed in the doorway to seal the tomb. The Gospels say it would take three or four people to move the stone. The religious authorities are concerned. Jesus has made comments in the Temple that he would be killed and on the third day, meaning Sunday, he would rise from the dead. In Tibetan it's called *chidak chomba*—many great beings of the past, just to demonstrate that they have overcome death, will rise from death. But, the authorities are concerned that Jesus' disciples might come in the night and roll away the stone and take the body, so they approach Pontius Pilate and ask for several guards, centurions, to be placed at the tomb, at least for a day or two.

Then the holy day starts—Friday night up to Saturday evening, the main holy day—and I think you can imagine how the disciples felt. They have gone into hiding together. They are staying in a safe house. They are very frightened: they saw what happened to Jesus from a distance. The Hill of Skulls, Golgotha—where the crucifixion took place—is plainly visible from the city walls and Jesus himself, as he died, could see the city he was hoping to help.

The disciples are in deep despair. They are weeping the whole night and the whole day, and I think that during that twenty-four hours something very powerful happens. It wasn't a miracle with Jesus, it was a miracle with his disciples. They look into their hearts, they realize they have failed their teacher, and they realize they have failed their own selves. They have the whole day—the rest of the city is celebrating the holiday, the greatest holiday of the year, and the disciples have the whole day to think about how their own teacher was killed, and they didn't try to help, and he warned them many times it would happen, and they were so selfish, so concerned about themselves, so concerned about how things would turn out for themselves.

I think on that Saturday, which was yesterday, they do a very powerful purification practice. You and I, we keep a diary of our bad deeds and our good deeds, and you know and I know that we are often busy and we do it in a sort of a lackadaisical way. We don't think about it too much. And maybe we've been doing it for years and we have still a pretty good karmic effect, but I believe that if you spent that Saturday with the disciples they have done more purification in the day than we have done in a year, or a whole lifetime.

The regret they must have felt was intense, to actually see your holy lama up dying, tortured and knowing you were too afraid to help, must have been very painful, and I think powerful. We call the four powers—regret—the way to stop bad karmic seeds. I think in those twenty-four hours each of the eleven left alive must have done a powerful purification.

Sunday morning dawns—that was this morning. Two of the women from the Galilean camp have wanted to prepare Jesus' body for proper burial in the old Jewish tradition. The body must be anointed in aloe oils and then the precious myrrh, the spice called myrrh, and it's said that this is why the three wise men, or kings, at Jesus' birth, one of them offered myrrh knowing what would become of him.

And so the two women—some gospels say three—but one of them is Jesus' mother, Mary, and the other woman is Mary Magdalene, a close devotee of Jesus. They couldn't go on Saturday to the tomb, because no work is allowed to be done, not even preparation of the body. So, they come with the spices and the aloe, and they are wondering how they'll get into the tomb, they will need several strong men to help.

When they reach the hill in which the tomb is dug, at the base of the hill they pass through a garden—some maybe olive trees—and they are amazed to see the stone is already rolled away.

The two Roman guards are lying there dazed. They're not hurt but they seem to be somehow almost in a trance. Mary, the mother of Jesus, and Mary Magdalene see a light coming out of the tomb. They are afraid, but they are both incredibly devoted to Jesus, and they put aside their fear and they come to the door of the tomb. Inside they see the linen cloth is there on the little bench, and there's no body, and there's an angel—a being of light, white light—the Bible says like lightning—and it's a young man.

They've never seen anything like this and they fall down on their knees, and they say, "Where's Jesus?" And the angel says, "Why do you look for a living man in the place where dead men are laid?"
Mary the mother is overjoyed. She's felt what any mother would feel and she runs as quickly as she can to the safe house where the eleven are hiding, to tell them what has happened. Mary Magdalene takes a few steps out of the tomb and falls down on the ground. The scriptures say that Jesus during his short time—it's only just over two years of teaching—he has this woman follower, extremely devoted,

maybe the most devoted follower, and he has cast devils out of her seven times. In the Bible, casting a devil out of a person is a word that refers to helping a person who is prone to very serious mental illness. It means every month or two this closest disciple has had major bouts of mental illness depression, anxiety—I think we can imagine she was almost intolerable, screaming—and the lama, Jesus, has seven times taken her out of it.

So she falls on the ground, I think she's maybe half crazy again, and she's weeping and screaming that the body has been taken. A man comes up behind her she looks up at him and she sees the gardener. He's a poor man; his job is to watch the olive trees, tend them, take care of them, and she is sobbing and she says, "Did you see who took the body? I must take care of the body! It's all we have left. Please tell me, who took the body?"

He stands a long time, quiet, then he looks at her and he says, "Mary," and she sees it's Jesus [*cries*]. Then she rises to hold him; he says, "Don't. Just go, run, tell the eleven I am alive. I will meet them in Galilee."

And so she runs. Mary the mother has already reached the house. They run into the room where the eleven are still crying and they say, "He's alive." And they say, "It can't be. You women are hysterical; you're upset. It can't be."

They don't even listen. Finally, Mary Magdalene convinces Peter to come and look. Out of the eleven he comes, and then it's over. He sees the cloth. It's time to go back to Galilee. Some of the disciples, two of them, are walking west of Jerusalem on a road. They are still weeping. A man comes up behind them, he says, "Why are you crying?"

They say, "Are you deaf? You haven't heard of what happened yesterday in Jerusalem? Jesus, the leader of so many people, was murdered."

He says, "That was supposed to be like that!"

They say, "What do you mean, supposed to be like that?"

Then, as they walk a long way the man debates with them, he argues with them.

He says, "All the scriptures say, the old scriptures, that the prophet who will come, will be murdered," and then he continues to quote the ancient books from memory.

The disciples are amazed that a normal man would know so much and then as they walk, he begins to show them that this is a part of a bigger plan, that this prophet must be killed for something bigger. They begin to approach a village; the disciples are hungry. They go to a place to eat. They ask the stranger to come with them. He says, "No, I must go on."

They beg him, "You have comforted us, you have such a knowledge. What you say, it seems like it could be true, that this was part of something more important."

He says, "All right, I will eat with you."

They go into a small inn. Bread is put on the table. The man reaches out and breaks the bread. The disciples are staring at his hands, the way he breaks the bread is exactly the way Jesus used to break it. They look up; they see Jesus [*cries*].

What is happening here, in the secret teachings is called *kyerim*. It is the first level of attainment of the secret teachings. It's obvious from these two events, and a later one with Peter when he is out in his boat near the Sea of Galilee, that these two, and three, men don't look like Jesus on the outside. People who have walked with Jesus for years, people who are his most devoted woman followers don't recognize him at first.

It means that outwardly these people couldn't have looked like Jesus, but the disciples' karma is so powerful, changing, and the two men are empty, and so they begin to see their teacher in other people. They begin to see the essence of an Enlightened Being beyond the form.

In the ancient Jewish law, in the tablets of Moses, one of the Ten Commandments is that you shouldn't even try to make an image of God. It is an incredibly powerful commandment. It means God doesn't have a physical form that you can fix. You can't say what divine being should look like. If you reach the higher levels of your spiritual life, the outer form becomes meaningless. You begin to see holy beings in every form. It is a high sign of karma having been cleaned.

When everyone here, all of us, are able to clean our karma enough, we will automatically, without effort, begin to meet holy bodhisattvas and enlightened beings in the people around us. I don't mean some kind of new-agey thing where you try to pretend that the people around you might be God or divine. I mean your karma has become so pure that you see it, and it's forced upon you, and you begin to become accustomed to living among holy beings, you are starting to enter heaven.

It doesn't happen in a day, it doesn't happen when you die. It happens now. It begins, and as long as your heart is becoming more and more pure, which is what our vows are supposed to help us do, then the people you see as Jesus, or whoever you feel will be the divine being, they become more and more around you.

I have seen people, we would meet them in New York City, they'd say, "I'm sort of interested in this stuff," and we'd say, "You must come and meet Khen Rinpoche. He's teaching this weekend. It's only a hour or two by bus."

And they would say, "I really don't have the time."

And so their perception of this holy priceless lama is of an ordinary sense—they really don't see him as anything special, not even worth a bus ticket. This is a proof that Holy Lama is empty; he doesn't have any nature. He's not a great lama or he's not a low lama, he's just empty. If you don't have good seeds in your heart you will see him as a normal person, and you'll say, "I'm busy this weekend."

And then other people who have more pure seeds in their crystal drop of consciousness, in their heart, they will hear Holy Lama's name and immediately ask, "Is there any chance to meet this holy being?" because of their seeds. And the empty lama they see as holy—before they even meet him. I had the honor to hear Lama's name. I was in India; I felt very attracted. I had a chance to meet His Holiness the Dalai Lama. I said, "I heard this lama's name, I'm thinking to study with him. What do you think?"

His Holiness said, "Do it."

But, you see then when people like that, they meet the people who don't think meeting this priceless holy being is worth a bus ticket, they look at those people and they feel sad for them. "Oh, this person doesn't have even the karma to meet Holy Lama once."

But then if our karmic seeds were really pure, if we worked very, very hard and sincerely, then we might be out in Saint David, Arizona and thirsty and ask, "Where's the nearest convenience store," and they say, "It's a ten-mile drive to Tombstone"—last I knew. And you go there and you pick up a soda and you put it on the counter and you look up and you see Khen Rinpoche [*cries*] in this lady at the counter.

If your seeds are pure enough it will start to happen. It's *kyerim*, and then you meet, maybe a person who is staying near Holy Lama—the version in New Jersey—and you say, "I saw Khen Rinpoche."

And they say, "In his room or on the lawn?"

And maybe it's hard to explain at that time about the lady in the convenience store. It means the seeds are starting to change in your mind.

So, the disciples go back to Galilee, according to some Gospels. They've gotten a message they should go to a certain mountain—something will happen. They assemble there, eleven, and Jesus appears to them. There's a long funny story I can't tell today. We don't have much time, and today we'll try to make the class shorter. We will only take one break and if you have to catch a plane or if it gets late, then I suggest after the break you sit near the door, and then you can slip out at the last minute. But I'll really try to finish much more quickly than before.

Jesus appears to the eleven. He says, "It's time to get to work."

They say, "What kind of work?"

He says, "It's time for you to teach people."

They say, "We'll try. Where? Where shall we teach people?"

Jesus says, "Jerusalem would be a nice place to start."

You can imagine how they feel *[laughs]*.

And he says, "One more thing before you leave: Don't take any money with you, you won't need it. The workman is worthy of his wages."

It means, if you serve the Dharma well, the wages will come to you. You don't have to ever worry about money if you truly go out into the world to serve others. You don't have to worry about place to stay or money what you're going to eat. Jesus says, "Don't worry, please, just forget it. You never have to worry."

And we never have to worry. If we dedicate our lives to serving others, what we need will certainly come. Lord Buddha said it countless times. He said it this way: "If a person in this tent who sincerely serves others, and goes out to serve, and teach others, if they should ever truly come into very hard circumstances then my Buddhahood is a lie and I am not a Buddha."

So you and I, we don't have to worry about those things; we can worry about countless other things but where the next meal will come from or where we will sleep, how we will live. If we go out to help others things will come, we shouldn't ever doubt Lord Buddha or worry about those things. Jesus says, "Don't take an extra pair of shoes, don't take an extra pair of clothes. Take one warm shawl. It's enough. No money." He says it directly.

I think here the disciples do one of the most courageous things in the Bible: they don't even hesitate, they're back on the road to Jerusalem. I think they have passed their test. I think their karma is clean now. Whatever karma they had of failing their teacher, doubting their teacher, failing to help or serve, they are resolved now. Things will be different. And so this huge failure of Jesus' mission in this moment is starting to become a piece of a bigger plan. And it's always like that.

Something much more powerful than Jesus wandering around Galilee teaching, is about to happen, out of the pain, out of the failure. The disciples have gained the most rare and precious spiritual quality of real humility. They have been humiliated by their own fear and weakness, and they admitted it fully. I don't think there was anyone among them who didn't cry the whole day on Saturday. They saw what they really were—you and I, we can't, we refuse—but they, I think they looked inside and they saw how badly they had failed and acted towards their teacher, and they regretted, and that regret removed the karma.

And so they walked back to Jerusalem bravely, proudly. There's another festival called *Shavuot,* it occurs fifty days after the festival of Passover. It's one of the three great festivals during which every Jewish male is expected to try to come to the Temple, make tribute, and at least be close to the extraordinarily holy place where Moses's tablets were once housed. The holiday in Greek is called Pentecost, because of fifty days.

The remaining eleven enter Jerusalem. Peter is up front, I believe he is with John or James. There's a beggar at the gate—you cross a small bridge and it goes into the gate in the wall. This beggar has been sitting in the same place for years; he has crippled broken, bent legs. He can't stand up. He holds out his hand to Peter, "Please give me something." Peter looks at him and says, "I don't have any money, but I'll give you something better. In the name of Jesus may you walk."

This is the highest form of a mantra. The disciples are beginning to develop the powers of the higher stages of the secret teachings. Because of the purity of his own heart, which came out of his true humility—having failed Jesus three times in one night as his teacher predicted—Peter is able to heal a person with a mantra. The most powerful of all mantras is your own heart lama's name. It doesn't work at all unless your own heart is pure.

The beggar gets up; he can walk. He doesn't just walk, he begins to dance all over the bridge. *[Laughs.]* People knew this beggar for years; people are amazed. "How did you do that? It's so wonderful!"

They go to Temple—word goes ahead of them like wildfire. People are dying to learn more. The city of Jerusalem is crowded again with pilgrims from all over the Mediterranean, anywhere where Jewish people have been taken as slaves over the last few thousand years. They still remain loyal to their faith and their teachers, and to the incredibly holy place in the temple where the divine has actually come to earth in the form of the tablets of Moses. And so the crowds form.

The *Sanhedrin,* the Council of Elders hears about it. "Trouble again, followers of Jesus, making trouble again." They take Peter and I believe John and James into custody.

"What are you doing?"

"We're just healing people."

"How do you do that?"

"We use the name of our heart lama."

The Sanhedrin just decides to beat them up and they send them away with a warning: "No more mention of this teacher. He has been killed already. If you do it again, you will be killed."

The eleven disciples hear about it. There's a twelfth disciple now, Matthias, having been chosen by the other eleven to make the full twelve, replacing Judas, who's dead. They say, "Sanhedrin, go to hell" *[laughs]*. They go to the Temple daily, they preach openly, bravely.

On the day of Pentecost, the holiday itself, the twelve are sitting in a special place near the temple, and each of them undergoes a transformation. Each begins to sing in a different language. Something overtakes them and each one begins to sing in a different language, languages they never heard of. People around them are amazed, someone says, "He is singing in Egyptian. This is the language of my home, this is where I come from." Another one says, "No, no. They are singing in Greek." Another one says, "No, it's Syrian." And each one begins to hear his own language.

This is a special power of the higher secret teachings of Buddhism. It's called the *sarva bhuta ruta jnanam* in Sanskrit. And people because of the purity of their karmic seeds, their inner channels of subtle energy begin to flow differently, and knowledge of all languages comes to them without any conscious effort.

The people are amazed and they want to know how this is happening. Suddenly, bursts of fire break out of the backs of the disciples, forking over their heads. This is also a very high sign of attainment in the secret teachings. Their channels are opening fully, they are achieving the highest goals of our own practice.

People are amazed, people begin to come to each of them, each learns in his own language about what Jesus was teaching. It's the same thing that Moses taught. People stopped listening after awhile. Moses had major trouble even in his own life later.

And then imagine after the Shavuot festival, three thousand people have become followers of these twelve men. Each one goes back to his own country, and in a hundred years these beliefs have spread over the whole world, because of the diaspora. And so this big failure, this big disaster has become something different, it becomes obviously something part of a greater plan that someone had.

uUw

We've been talking each day about a good karma that you and I may have done that we could give away to other people, because this is what the chapter by Master Shantideva is about. I think it's my joyful duty to remind you of the good karma I have seen you do. I so often pick on you. It's only fair. I would like to speak today about all the hard work I've seen all of you doing to help the teachings in this world. I would like to speak about all the amazing things you have done to make sure that these teachings survive in this world and that people who wish to have a chance to drink of these teachings.

We're not allowed or encouraged in Buddhism to proselytize, bother people, but if people are interested, if people see an announcement for a talk and think it might be interesting and come of their own accord, then it's our responsibility and it's our great honor to have something ready for them. There are people sitting here, they came to the very first tiny classes—five, six, seven people—and this man had the wisdom to bring a tape recorder. He said, "I'd like to remember what's said," even to the first class I think, "and maybe later someone might want to know what was said." He kept bringing a tape recorder to class.

People would ask him, "Did you get that third class? I missed it." He would make a tape for them, and now it's been, I think about ten years later. He continued to insist that these tapes should be made. He spent a great deal of his own time, countless hours, and a great deal of his own money. He got better and better tapes made, he made them into beautiful packages. People in other states and other cities began asking for them. He made sure everyone got what they needed. There was a big sign, and I hope there still is, on the front of the package that said, "If you don't have any money, don't worry about it—it's free."

And now I heard—I saw, illegally—a small pamphlet in the temple library that over 75,000 tapes have been distributed from the kindness of this person. You have assured that the first great introduction of the great holy books of our lineage and tradition, which Khen Rinpoche so kindly imparted to us, are available to anyone who wishes. I have gone around the world teaching—I've seen tapes everywhere.

People come up to me: "What's your name?"

"I'm Geshe Michael."

"Yeah, but do you know John Stilwell? For years I've been listening to the tapes and his questions on the tapes, they're amazing! And he was so kind, he wrote me a letter, sent me everything I needed. We have a small group now, we are all listening to them, I teach them sometimes to others."

This is going on all over the world. This is an incredible service to the teachings. Each box of tapes comes with the original scriptures and the translation. And there are many people here who worked very hard to make tapes. We offered to people could write back, and send questions, or homework and we tried very hard to have a small group of people answer their questions, check their homeworks. It was extremely difficult. There were thousands of papers. People in prisons—a big network developed—people would send in ten-page letters about their life as an answer to a simple question *[laughs]* and kind students in New York would carefully answer each letter. It was all done at night in people's free time.

And then young people, really sincere, devoted good young people came, started saying, "I can help, I want to learn to translate. I want to learn how to make these notebooks. I can help you." It's normally a long road to become a translator, but these people were so sincere, they worked so hard, we had several very good teachers of Tibetan helping and within a few years they were producing very beautiful translations. Some of the parts of the courses were translated by them. Almost all of the Tibetan was checked, printed, laid out by them. Oftentimes they spent all night working. Now, in retreat and elsewhere, people continue to translate. I think you'll be very happy later. Those who are prepared will be able to read many of the secret teachings in English.

One retreatant is working on an ancient commentary to our practice. Another retreatant is working on another commentary. They have made very good progress. We are already using those commentaries. A third young retreatant has translated all the beautiful secret rituals, for example, the beautiful fire offering that we do, and all this retreat we have used her translations for our special offering ceremonies.

Other people, one of the caretakers in particular, produced... I checked the other day, just so I would tell the right thing. It's about 800 pages, a manuscript of the entire teachings of a great lama of about 200 years ago, on our retreat practices. There's another person here—I think—took all the tapes, recordings of all the classes we all took together in India, Sera Monastery, spent over two years carefully transcribing them out, adding all the Tibetan in pronunciation, and has made two beautiful books of the extraordinary teachings we received on emptiness and the Mind-Only. There's not more than a handful of clear explanations in the whole world in any language of this difficult and important subject. This man has saved this extremely precious knowledge for all of us to share, and continues to help people with the tapes, and I think you will study this subject from him.

There are people in New York who came and said, "I will make books out of the teachings." They spent years making beautiful manuscripts. We couldn't finish them before retreat, but there are three or four extraordinary manuscripts done by several very fine writers. One Indian woman especially, did the Mahamudra teachings, and a couple who are very fine poets and writers have prepared several other manuscripts.

We were approached by a large book company to write several books about Buddhism. They came out with my name on them, but you should know that they were a collaboration by several holy students here who didn't even want their names on the book.

People here have worked very hard to make the teachings available to others. There's a man here who spent years trying to finalize the preparations for *Godstow Retreat Center*. This is a large and very expensive estate property which was donated for a dollar to our organization, but there were major problems in the final papers and things to do with the deeds and, and the township, and the zoning, and this man took all the responsibility because he had a vision that people might do retreats in this place for many, many years to come. There was a woman, a lawyer who spent countless hours working on this project, and she and her husband spent countless hours working on the house and the grounds, and it's due to her kindness that we are able to serve others in this center.

Then in New York fifteen senior students came forth and said, "I will help teach." They underwent training for about a year and a half, specially. Then they began to teach others. It's very difficult to teach people in your own country if you're not Tibetan or Indian, if you don't have a red robe or a yellow robe on, if your head's not shaved or very long hair. People think you're just a normal person. It's very hard, even if you're very knowledgeable, to teach your peers.

I was in India, at Gyalrong college, our college, the best in the universe, and they led in an old man one day, an old, a very old monk, and they ran to me and they said, "Venerable has escaped from Tibet."

Every year we get between fifty and a hundred new refugees, many of them badly injured during the escape, many die in the attempt.

He shuffled in. I spoke to him for a while. People said, "This is Khen Rinpoche's classmate from Tibet. He just escaped." And I spoke to him; I was overjoyed. They said, "This is the last classmate alive of Khen Rinpoche's."

And I spoke with him and he said, "Young feller, you speak pretty good Tibetan there!" and, "How'd you learn that?"

And I said, "Holy Lama Khen Rinpoche taught me most of the things I know."

He said, "Oh what's his name?"

I said, "He's the great former abbot who's living in America." (In Tibetan it's *Ari Khensur Rinpoche*).

He said, "Yeah yeah, but what's his name?"

And I said, "His holy name is Geshe Lobsang Tharchin."

He said, "Lobsang Tharchin, that sounds familiar."

I said, "Well they tell me he was your classmate."

And he looks up, he says, "Oh Lobsang Tharchin? That little goofball? I don't believe a word of what you say, he could never teach nobody! Last time I saw him he was putting thumbtacks out on the pathways around the monastery buildings"— because monks used to walk barefoot—"He was the biggest cutup in our whole class. He can't be the Khen Rinpoche you're talking about."

I said, "Venerable, how long ago was that?"

He said, "Oh, just a while back maybe, oh god, it's been seventy years now!"

He couldn't believe that this goofball had become abbot of Sera Mey and the greatest lama to teach all the westerners, and this is called a "peer perception problem." Anyone here who tries to become a teacher, you will run into it. People will say, "I knew Winston when he was back just starting. He can't be teaching. He can't be explaining *drange* to people, I knew him back when!"

And it happens all over the world. Geshe Thubten Rinchen's classmates commonly tell me, "Oh, he's just a kid!" The abbot of Gyumey Tantric College was debating with us in the debate ground. It seems just a while back.

And you have to overcome this problem. It always happens like that. You don't appreciate the teachers who have worked so hard, you don't really respect a person who comes from your own country. Sakya Pandita said a wise man is never appreciated in his own hometown. Jesus was thrown out of Nazareth's synagogue. He was almost killed when he tried to teach there. But you have to teach. This is a lineage. It happens every generation, the other students think, "You're just a kid, you were in the same class as me." But that's how the next generation starts. And I'm really proud—I think we've done it the right way—the teaching has now passed to the next generation. You have worked very hard, you have trained yourself as well as any monk ever did in Tibet and I tell you frankly, better than 95 percent of them. You are qualified, you are ready to teach, and you are teaching, and you must teach. You must go on teaching, the new generation of teachers has come. And this is the way it must be if we are to help many people.

People here who are training, who have been training, who have gone to many classes who have done much personal retreat, contemplation, work on your own heart—you must now begin to teach. And I heard rumors sometimes the teachers who come and help us with their own sweet knowledge, holy teachers, some of them here, very great and kind teachers who come and help us, it will slip out of their mouth, "Oh, so-and-so was teaching in Ireland," and I've heard that three of you at least have been helping people in Ireland. This is incredibly good karma because it's the survival of the lineage.

The lineage is going on. The lineage has passed to the next generation. This is a wild success of our work. I'm very honored and proud. It's a very frightening thing to think that after two and a half thousand years the lineage would stop in the

United States, or other western countries. It must pass on. You are doing perfect, beautiful work. I couldn't be more happy. You have made me, you have made your teacher, and all your teachers are extremely happy, because you are saving the Dharma. Your teaching, your working to teach others, is breathing the life into the Dharma for the next generation.

I know that some of the staff, the caretakers, are teaching here also, in this area. It's a wonderful thing. I've heard beautiful things from people. I know that people are teaching in New York and, I think, Godstow. Some of the teachers who come to us have blurted out things about how beautiful those classes are. It's a wonderful thing.

I was in India, I was in Sera; we were learning from Geshe Thubten Rinchen. A small group of people came to me. They said, "We're your grandchildren." I said, "That's not possible." They said, "No, you don't understand; we're from Australia and we've been studying with a holy lama there"—a sweet, wonderful Australian man

We got a fax from this crazy man about, I don't know, six, seven years ago. He had seen the Diamond Cutter Sutra, a video, and he said, "We have to bring this to Australia!" He worked very hard and it went to Australia, and then he began to teach. I asked him, I begged him—he's too modest—to teach, and he has wonderful students. You don't know what it feels like to have people come up to you and say "I have been taught by the people you taught," because it means that the work of your whole life has been meaningful *[cries]*. So, I beg you to continue. You have to prepare the next generation—then you will have the same pleasure of meeting your own grandchildren later in strange places.

I'd like to make it clear today I would be very pleased if each of the people who have taken a major responsibility—the director of ACI in New York, the director of Diamond Mountain, the director of the Asian Classics Input Project, trying to save the holy books, those of you who have taken responsibility to teach in other states, or other countries—I would like to make it very clear that I consider the lineage to be passed on. It's my hope even after three-year retreat, that you will continue to serve as you serve, in the capacities which you are serving.

I pray, and I beg you on behalf of all of us living teachers, that you continue your work and you pass it on to the next generation, and you take special care to find suitable special people to whom you can pass on these responsibilities when the time is right for you, when the three-year retreat bug bites you.

I would love to continue to teach special classes, especially for people who are prepared. I long to instruct a handful of really fine translators more than I've been able to do. I think Arizona's a good place to work with special classes, and I think Diamond Mountain will be a special university for teachers.

I think New York City is an incredible place. I think some of the most talented people in the world have the karma to pass through New York City. I would be—if it's the wish of people, or the boards of the places in New York and Connecticut—I would love to come for special teachings maybe a few times, few months out of the year.

And then maybe I, and Christie, we have serious practices we must finish. We are truly trying to reach the highest goals of these teachings. We are working incredibly hard. I think it's important for a teacher to set an example and try very hard to reach the final goals of the highest teachings of our lineage, and so I would also like to continue some deep retreats, but not all at once.

And, I think, I would be very pleased to continue to teach special classes or events like an elder statesman. I think the primary teaching of the eighteen courses should be the responsibility of the directors and the board. There should be strong boards in New York, and Connecticut, and Diamond Mountain, and you people here must take responsibility that those teachings remain and are healthy. It's been passed on to you now and it's your responsibility to train yourselves well. It's your serious obligation now to carry that baby to the next generation.

And I will teach many wonderful classes also. I can't stop my mind wandering during retreat, and I have many ideas for advanced special courses, and we're working very hard. One of the people who is helping a lot to design courses on the higher teachings is here, I think, I don't know for sure. He is the director of the Asian Classics Input Project. They—he and two sweet holy beings who have worked so hard for many years—they are both named…in the monastery they call them "Bowb"—"Bowb and Bowb"—they have worked very hard. You have that good karma to dedicate to other people.

"What good karma?"

The ancient books in Tibet were burned during the invasion in the 1950s and '60s and '70s. Thousands and thousands and thousands of books were destroyed. The woodblocks were used as a joke to parquet the floors of military buildings. Tibetan people were required to walk on their holy scriptures. And now those things are almost lost. But there are huge collections still in Russia; there are two huge collections in Mongolia; and the people under Holy John Brady have worked very hard.

I want to tell John Brady a story; you have to pass it on. I don't think I've ever told any of you.

Around 1985 I went to a university. I was taking classes from a professor of Sanskrit, Holy Lama Samuel Atkins, and he was a great Greek scholar. He took me in the basement, and there was a whole desk covered with odd computer pieces and it was the first CD-ROM. The owner of Hewlett-Packard, David Packard, Jr., was there. He's a Greek scholar and they had spent, I think about 15 million dollars, to type in the ancient Greek scriptures and literature, in Korea and the Philippines. I saw all of the knowledge of Greek literature in a single little shiny piece of plastic.

He told me, Mr. Packard, this will be the future of computers. These things will be able to hold the whole literature of a single culture in one or two diskettes. I was… you know what I was thinking! I went home; we started to type, me and a guy named Robert Lacey. In a year we had finished a fifty-page book. Then a great man named Ngawangthondup Narkyid—he is the greatest Tibetan linguist in the world, he is the biographer of the Dalai Lama, he lives with His Holiness—every day he writes down what His Holiness has done that day. He's on volume 58 or something. He's pretty old now, but I told him, "We have this dream, we would like to put the *Kangyur* and the *Tengyur*—our holy books, four and a half thousand books, a million pages—we would like to put them onto these special disks and give them to everyone for free."

He said, "Extraordinary!" He said, "Say that into this tape recorder," and we sat down and we made a tape for His Holiness. And Kuno-la is his name, special name, he took the tape to His Holiness *[cries]* and we got a message back that said, "Please try to do it." I recently got an illegal message—they just come in the lunch box, Christie reads them, and I refuse, and she tells me what they say—and it said, "It looks like we've finished the Kangyur and Tengyur."

It's almost twenty years of work, hundreds of Tibetan refugees have been trained, helped, and many monks have worked. There are many Tibetan refugee women working and you should know, John, you should tell the others that His Holiness's dream has been fulfilled. Someone should tell His Holiness. *[Laughs.]*

We offered His Holiness almost the whole thing a few years back; he was extremely pleased. So this is another example of a lineage. These people took over this work. John didn't know *ga* from *ka*, but he agreed to take it over. The project, as usual, was in debt. There were large salaries that were owed to refugees, very embarrassing, hard to admit. They kept going; they refused to stop; they didn't get paid. I left it like that for John—like so many things. He took it over happily, and it's extraordinary work. In Russia and Mongolia, I believe, over 100,000 books have been checked, and catalogued, and a free catalog made for everyone in the world. And the diskettes of the scriptures are given to everyone for like a dollar or fifty cents. This hasn't been done in the last thousand years. The last person to try to finish Kangyur and Tengyur was the seventh Dalai Lama. He had a thousand woodcarvers working for thirty years.

And then recently, people in places like this and Godstow have made sure that people could start doing long-term retreats. You are passing on the teachings of Lord Buddha in this important way.

I hope that the people in charge of the retreat centers will continue to work hard to provide retreat places for people. You should know that the retreatants have worked very hard to prepare materials for people who do long retreats in the future. One of the holy people sitting up here has prepared an hour-and-a-half script of visualizations, what to do each few seconds as you go through the sadhana, how to visualize each step. She worked on it for almost two years now. And another retreatant worked very hard to produce a manual of problems we have run into in retreat and solutions that we have worked out by necessity. Another retreatant has gone through the entire sadhana and illustrated it in very beautiful way and continues to work hard to make even more beautiful illustrations.

There are people here who are working—I think if he's here, Mr. Ted Lemon, I don't know *[laughs]*, they are working to make a dictionary from the several thousand pages of translations that have been done by the other people here. It will be online, I think it's online perhaps already, but you can just type in the word you don't know, and it will jump you to the ancient book where that word was used in its most important way, and there are large numbers of people working on that. One of the retreatants was the pioneer who started that project. I wish you well. I hope you will work for a lineage of people who continue this work.

And so all of you, you have this extraordinary good karma. Even talks like this have come out, people working hard making books. People went to Mongolia, I believe one of the…I shouldn't say one, I should say the person in Mongolia who had the idea to bring teachings to hundreds of thousands of Mongolians. This man just appeared, I guess, after a talk one day. He said, "I'll take responsibility. You just send people here to speak, I'll make sure that everyone knows."

Tens of thousands of people attended those talks. Hundreds of thousands of people saw them on Mongolian television. This is one single man's dream, one man's vision. And he worked without any support. None of these people ever got paid, or if they did it was worked out to ten cents an hour or something. But, he has done extraordinary work to spread the teachings.

There are people here who taught even special private small groups in New York, meditation every morning before work. And I believe that every person here has been a teacher around a coffee table somewhere, teaching people the best way, quietly, privately, one on one, two on one. They're asking questions about these ideas, karma, what's emptiness, and you have been teaching many thousands of people.

You have this karma. This kind of transfer of the holy Dharma from one country to another hasn't happened in a thousand years. Lord Buddha predicted that this transfer would occur at this time. You know if you studied the Diamond Cutter. You are in the middle of the transfer of the greatest knowledge of mankind to one of the most influential countries, several of them, in the world. People in this country and other western countries, many people really want to know these things.

Anyone who's suffering, anyone who's had a friend or a loved one die, is questioning how these things happen. You have the knowledge. You're opening the window from the holy lamas of Tibet and India, Mongolia, and you're letting those ideas come into this country. You have extraordinary good karma. You think you're just a few wacky people. You think it's just a few little Dharma books or tapes—it's not like that. Ideas which can prevent people's death, ideas which can prevent people's suffering forever are entering our culture, because people like you are working so hard. You can't dream of the effects that your actions are having for the future. You are like the disciples of Jesus in Jerusalem sitting around a dusty little temple and you are teaching a few people. You have no idea what will happen. It won't be limited to this world. It will go beyond even this planet. You are sitting at a crux in time. The karma you have in your mind is intense. It will continue to grow.

People who work on the books, to save the books: you can't imagine the books that will come to you yourself in a few years, just drop out of the sky—books you've never dreamed of, instructions for places no one has much gone to—because of your work. These things will start to happen to you. You have to take care of those beautiful seeds in your mind. How? First try to crystallize them. When you go home tonight think, "I'm sitting at a moment in history. I'm sitting at the window. Ideas which could help millions of people are passing through my hands."

It's extraordinary. You have to give away those karmas. On a dry cement level you can make books, hand them around, help people, talk to people. On a half-dry cement level, you can bring these projects up to a certain stage, and then as they approach their goals, you give them away. You give the credit and the karma of the finishing to other people—this is bodhisattva's way of life.

And then on a deep level, deep inside the crystal drop of consciousness in your heart—you must look inside, you must imagine incredibly powerful karmic seeds like neutrons about to explode into an atom bomb, and you have to try to give them away to other people with your own thoughts, with the power of your own concentration, with the power of your meditation. You are then working at the causal level.

The results of your prayers, results of your dedication, will touch countless planets. You can't believe it, you don't really believe what I say, but I beg you to try. Work at the causal level. Even just imagine those karmas I mentioned, that you have done and continue to do, and go into them. Work hard—imagine them. In your mind give them away. Give away every sweet thing you have done.

Please remember one thing: those karmas don't expire. Every time you remember a good thing you did, another karma is planted. You can reinvest this karma—like my old diamond company boss—just by being happy about the incredible things you've done. It could be ten years ago; it doesn't matter. If you just remember and are happy about something you've done, extraordinary new karmas grow in your mind. Then you think about them and you give them away. And you think about the pleasure and happiness of giving them away, and they grow bigger.

It's a blissful path to bliss, says Master Shantideva. Please remember these methods. This is working at the level of what has created our universe itself.

There's another holy practice, called a hug. I'll tell you the secret way. You put your arms around a person. It might the guy who made the tapes in the beginning. It might be the guy who has the headache of this incredibly beautiful tent and these teachings, who has worked so hard with his wife. It might be the caretakers who have devoted their whole lives to extraordinary service. You can't imagine the service we receive. We are ashamed to know people are working so hard and so beautifully. It's like living in a paradise already. I'm not exaggerating and I'm not just being complimentary. It's true, and every retreatant knows it.

You can hug the guy who just finished the Kangyur and the Tengyur—probably knows *ga* from *ka* by now. You can hug the guy who's trying to run Godstow. You can hug the guy who's creating a dictionary that people can use for centuries. You can hug all the people who help so hard here and other places to serve the dharma. You can hug that lama from Australia. You can embarrass the sweet Mongolian man who reached out to hundreds and thousands of others.

I probably forgot a few holy beings here, so I think it's wiser—you can hug the teachers who have come here to help us—it's probably safer to hug everybody. When you put your arms around them, you touch their back between their shoulder blades where their heart is, and you imagine that you're touching their holy crystalline drop of consciousness. Then when you put your chest up to their chest you imagine that you dedicate to them all the holy power of the good deeds you have done, even just in the last few days—I know they have been long.

Don't waste any opportunity. In the highest teachings we don't touch another human being without thinking of the deep channels of energy and sending through the power of our thought energy into their channels. So a hug is not a simple thing. Every time you touch another person at all you have to remember the crystal drop in your heart. It's a very holy practice to open that drop and send your crystal good karmas into the heart of other person. Whack them on the back.

So I'd like you to do that practice now while you have refreshments, and then we'll try to finish sort of quickly. One thing: it doesn't hurt to whisper in their ear, "I'd like to get in on that good karma you're doing. Can I help you? Can I serve you? I heard you do the Kangyur, Tengyur. Did Geshe Michael tell you there's a hundred thousand more books to do? I know you might need some help. I'd like to help."

So, if there are people here who if something sounded exciting to you then try to meet the person, give them a hug, and offer them your help, OK?

[Break]

Okay, we'll fly through the rest of the dedication chapter so you can fly. First verse please.

John Brady:

(31) **And by this goodness I have done**
May every single suffering being
Give up every single harmful
Thought or word or deed;
Taking up always in its stead
Thoughts and words and deeds of virtue.

This is a very joyful section of the chapter. Master Shantideva will be describing the process by which you get a gardener to turn into Jesus. Or a guy you meet on the road. Or a lady behind the counter at the 7-Eleven in Tombstone—I guess a lot of people will go tonight *[laughs]*.

Whether you see Jesus or Khen Rinpoche in that lady is up to your good karma. Master Shantideva is dedicating his book that people who have been doing harmful things to others, and saying not so kind things to others, and thinking not very nice things about others, that they should all change now and begin to think of sweet thoughts of others.

It's not a naïve thought. Other people are often irritating. Other people harm us. Other people do plenty of bad things to us. That's no argument. But, if we react with hatred or dislike, or if we try to hurt them, then we only cause more bad people to come to us in the future.

Master Shantideva is the master of patience—the art of not getting angry. He's not naïve. We have created a mess around us, each of us. There will be people and situations that we'd rather not have come to us. But, if we respond with compassion and grace—force where it's necessary, if it's for something good—then we can change normal people into holy beings around us. So, the first step is to clean up our own karmic act. Second verse:

Angela Lawlor *(In Irish—as Gaeilge)*:
> **Nach n-éireoidh gach duine as an streachailt chun**
> **An príomhaidhm a bhaint amach, ar son an chine daonna;**
> **Agus go liofí a gcroíthe le tuile**
> **An dea-iompar agus an ghrá.**
> **Go bhfagfaidh siad ar lár an droch-iompar,**
> **Agus go bhfanfaidh siad I gcuram an Duine Naofa.**

[Laughter and applause from Geshe-hla.] You have 57 verses to translate!

(32) **May these beings never cease to strive**
To reach the ultimate goal, for others;
And may their hearts be swept away
By the stream of loving conduct.
May they abandon every sort of dark behavior,
Remaining in the care of every Holy Being.

[More laughter and applause.] You don't have to go to 7-Eleven. That's good. I forget the verse. Master Shantideva gives us the second item in the list of ammunition you need to see Jesus in other people, and I'm not talking poetically, I mean real thing. You need simply to have kindness for other people. It's not hard. Everyone in the world is suffering. Everyone in the world is unhappy with something. Everyone in the world is on their way to death and afraid. It doesn't take an effort to feel sad for everyone else. There's no powerful person, or confident person, or strong person you've met who's not afraid. So, it's not hard to really be concerned for them and when you, when we break down the wall, it's much more fun and happy to serve others. It's a lot more fun.

I have tried in a small way to serve others. I fail very often. But I was introduced to these holy ideas when I was young, and a small amount has sunk in. And I can honestly say that if you spend even a small amount of your time trying to serve others you will be incredibly happy all the time and unbelievable things will happen to you.

Then Master Shantideva mentions the code of sweet loving conduct. This is a bodhisattva's code, six perfections. He's sending his karma to people to learn kindness, and how to express that kindness. Then he says, "May people abandon dark behavior;" in Tibetan it's *du kyi le*. *Du* means "a devil, demons"; *le* means "their work". *Du kyi le* means "May the sweet people around us never be captured by the devil."

What would it be like to be captured by the devil? It only means one thing in our lineage, in our teaching: It means to be caught by selfishness. It means to stop thinking about others. It means to focus on what we want, on our own needs. This is poison. This is a dead end. This is the way to be unhappy every minute of the day.

It's such a simple thing. Just don't worry about yourself. Things will come that you need, more than you ever dreamed of. Try to be in the embrace of the enlightened ones—it means try to spend your whole day in that warmth thinking about what other people need. It's a liberation in itself. Even if all this karma and emptiness stuff is not true, just the simple act of serving others is a true happiness. Next verse.

Susan Schwartz:

(33) **May every living soul enjoy**
A life immeasurably long,
Living thus forever in
A state of constant bliss,
So that even the very word "death"
Is never heard spoken again.

I tried to teach these ideas for many years. Many people told me, frankly, "I like you. You seem to be sincere. But this constant mention that people could escape death itself, I haven't heard that said a lot in books, I've read about Buddhism and I haven't heard people talk like that much, and I appreciate that you seem to believe it, but I don't really think it's possible."

If things are empty, if things don't have a nature of their own, if the reality around us is a product of that tiny crystal drop of consciousness in our hearts, then by changing defects in the DNA of the small crystal—the karmas—your body and my body can change into the body of an angel.

The stories throughout history of angels are not foolish talk. Those angels didn't come from nowhere. The many mentions of heaven in all the literature of every culture are not just fancy stories. We can go there, because the world around us is empty, if we can try to be good to others.

And it's not hard. You don't have to be like John Brady, or John Stilwell, or Winston, or Salim Bhai, or Batbold. You don't have to save the world. All you need is to be kind, truly kind, truly think of the people right around us. And then your world will start to change into a paradise, and your body will change.

There will come a day when all of us will be sitting around at Diamond Mountain, a campfire, cooking marshmallows, and somebody will say, "I was reading an old book."

"Yeah?"

"And there's this word in there, I can't figure it out."

"What is it?"

"It's 'death.'"

"I don't know. I think we used to know that word, but forgot what it means now."

And Master Shantideva is saying outright there will come a day when the word "death" is not known in this world. We have to try to make it happen. People like you and me have to work very hard on ourselves, and we have to work hard to serve others with this knowledge, and then death will vanish from the world. Next verse please.

Carolyn Christie:

(34) **May all the places that exist, in every world there is,
Turn instantly into gardens of elegant design,
Filled with trees that grant your every wish.
And may the Enlightened Ones, along with their daughters
And their sons, walk amidst the trees,
Singing out the sweet song of the Dharma.**

It's a special word in Tibetan here, called *kyemoy tsel*—*kyemo* means "something grown," *tsel* means "a garden." There are two kinds of gardens in ancient India. One would just be a corner of a forest that a king liked to hang around in, and the other would be when some person had come in, a gardener, maybe Jesus, would come in and shape the trees into beautiful shapes, and cut the hedges into beautiful shapes, and they would go out and find deer and bring them to the garden. And this is what they call a man-made garden.

All of us are engaged in the in the act of trying to create our own garden. It's a powerful word he's using. We have to create our own paradise by being good to others. In that paradise there will be the wish-giving tree. This is a special tree, *paksam gyi shing*. It's like Aladdin's lamp. You say, "I'd like a maple-covered doughnut." And *pop!*—it just grows out of the tree and you pick it off and you eat it, if you can get away with it *[laughs]*.

It's an image for kindness. You can get anything you want if you are kind. All things will come to you, I repeat, we will all be going out to help others. There will be hard times—I don't think as bad as the disciples, many of whom died from being stoned to death, or executed, or crucified themselves, even out of those twelve. But, we may have hard times, but we don't have to worry. There's a balance between living a long time in a well-fed body, and maybe living a little shorter time in a badly-fed body, but to be serving others with it—it's a easy choice to make, I think.

So, Master Shantideva is saying, and I hope the lady from 7-Eleven or some other country, is walking through those gardens with her sons and daughters. The sons and daughters in the verse are bodhisattvas and bodhisattvis. And he's saying that if your heart is clear—and it takes time—one by one the people around you, you will see as Jesus. I repeat, the early disciples who saw Jesus today, Sunday, he didn't look like Jesus at first, and then they saw the real being behind the form because their hearts were cleaned by the humility of failing. Next verse please.

Keith Horan:

(35) And in each one of these places
May the very foundation, the earth itself,
Be transformed, from sharp stones and the like,
Into the heavenly ground of lapis lazuli—
As smooth as the palm of your hand,
And soft to walk upon.

[Laughs at Irish accent.] It's great to hear the Mother Tongue. And it's very good to have you here.
This is a reference to descriptions of paradise in the old books. The ground is been replaced. There's no more sharp stones, or cactuses, rattlesnakes *[laughs]*. It's all like beautiful lapis, dark blue with golden shimmering sparks in it, and even though it looks like crystal, when you step on it it's like—they say like foam rubber, really. It sinks under your step and it bounces back up. It's a metaphor for the way the world will become.

If you try to be kind to others, if you work hard, especially in ultimate ways—in the very cause of the universe—in your own drop of consciousness, if you try hard to give away your good deeds to others, from heart to heart, your world itself, the outer world, will begin to change. It's a wonderful feeling. It's indescribable happiness. And it's not such a big deal to be nice to others, it's more fun. They need things; we have them; we give them. Everyone comes out a winner. And the world begins to change into extraordinarily beautiful place for you.

You have to try to cause that. You have to, tonight, please, in the next few weeks and months. It's a beautiful practice. I know we're all busy with many good practices. It's important not to overload yourself with good practices because then you get crazy.

But decide on a time, drop another good practice for a while and just sit back, enjoy some beautiful thing you've done. Crystallize it in your heart simply by thinking about it, and then send it away to help someone else. Imagine it going into their own heart. It's an easy, beautiful practice, and it is working with the very causes of our universe. Try it tonight. Drop another practice for a while. Ten, fifteen minutes on this practice. It's a joyful practice. You can't say you don't have any good deeds—I think we covered everyone here in the last four days. Next verse.

David Life:
(36) **And like a precious jewel**
Adorning this same ground,
May all the secret worlds that exist
And all the goodness in them
Abide atop these newfound lands,
Crowded with Warrior Angels.

[Laughs.] You've heard the word mandala. There are many kinds of mandalas. We offer a mandala before the teaching. That mandala is our imagination of a world which is perfect, and we offer it for the teaching. At the end of the teaching we offer all the people in the universe living in a perfect world as a thank-you for the teaching.

There are painted mandalas and there are sand mandalas. All of the retreatants have learned to make the special mandala for our practice. Several of them have done very beautiful manuals to help people in the future learn to make these special, perfect worlds. And I know that many of the staff of Diamond Mountain and other places have also been keeping this practice.

But this mandala, secret world, that Master Shantideva is talking about is a perfect world—you can imagine it as floating above our world. Our world is ordinary suffering. Our world is a lot of pain. Our world is inevitable old age and death. And above it floats a perfect world, and Master Shantideva is saying, "By the power of kindness, may the mandala descend into this world, and this world becomes the mandala."

If you understand emptiness, then there's no problem with this world becoming a kingdom of heaven. This world doesn't come from its side, it comes from us. It comes from the me—small subtle seeds in your own heart—and if you could change those seeds by being kind and helpful to others then this world would change into the kingdom of heaven or you can call it mandala or paradise—it's all the same place. Next verse please.

Sharon Gannon:
(37)	And too, may all who live and breathe
Hear the song of birds,
The wind in the trees,
The light of the sun, and the sky itself,
Singing aloud to them an endless
Rhapsody of holy teachings.

Just as a gardener or a guy on the street can turn into Jesus for you, any event around you can turn into the teaching of an enlightened being, when our hearts are clear enough, clean enough, when the karmic seeds are pure enough. And you can make it happen much faster by giving away your good karmas, hugging lots of people *[laughs]*—then something amazing happens. Even the wind in a tree can teach you these holy sweet teachings.

I like to sit near the ocean, especially in a certain sacred island, and listen to the waves coming in, and if our hearts are pure enough we can hear the Buddhas teaching. Even sunlight coming down, touching our bodies, we can hear it as the sweet teachings of enlightened beings. If a black and white stick can appear to you as a pen, because your mind is forming it into a pen, and if a gardener can appear to be a divine being to a person who has enough faith—she's been through terrible times—then it's no problem for the sound of the waves, or the sound of the wind, or the sunlight to sing to us the teachings of the enlightened beings. Next verse please.

Brian Smith (Ven. Marut):
(38)	And wherever they go may they always meet
The Enlightened Ones, and their children
Who strive for enlightenment.
May they honor these Lamas—
The highest of beings—
With endless showers of offerings.

He's talking about, he sends his good karma to people, "May they run into enlightened beings and then may they make offerings to these beings."

I would like to give you a very personal instruction. It's very dear to me. There will come a day when your heart is so clean from giving away your goodness that you will, for the first time, meet a person and see them as a holy being. If you have the seeds to see Jesus, if that's what a holy being is to you, you will see Jesus. If it's seeds to see a different form of holy being, you will see that being.

Because your heart is only just barely pure enough, it will waver. It will come in and out of holiness. "I think this is Vajra Yogi…uh, no."

And then suddenly, "I think so," and then, "Maybe not." But you will have doubt. The doubt itself is a terrible bad karma. It is an evil karma. It is the greatest evil that there is.

When the time comes and you stand before a person and they say something, and it flashes through your mind for an instant, "This could be Her," "This could be Him," you have to stop, get down on your knees, put your head at their feet.

They will say, "What the hell you doing, guy?" If you doubt at that moment they will disappear. They will become a surprised offended stranger.

At that moment you must redouble your faith. "Don't talk to me like that, Vajra Yogini. Don't talk to me like that, Jesus, I know who you are. You can't make me doubt. Have this doughnut, I've been saving it."

Strange things will happen. Your karma is—you see, I'm being serious—your karma is not strong, it's fragile, to see them. It will slip in and out of the ordinary to the divine. And through the strength of your faith you have to hold on. They might hit you. They might accuse you of being a bad person. They might say you're crazy. They might throw you out of their home. But never doubt them. Then you will begin to see them more and more. Make offerings to them. Believe who they are and the faith will cause the reality to change. When the time comes you have to be ready. Next verse please.

Bernie McGonagle:
(39)   **May the lords of the sky**
        Send down the rains on time,
        So to bring forth plentiful harvests.

> **May all existing governments**
> **Make their decisions based on the teachings,**
> **And thus may the whole world prosper.**

[Laughs.] Master Shantideva is finishing his chapter. There will be three verses now, I think which are general prayers for the whole world. In Tibet they believe that rain was sent down by local gods. Small gods—not enlightened beings, but local spirits—and he's praying that they should send the rains down for all the earth, and that governments throughout the world should begin to change.

Again the very weather, the state of the crops in the whole world, the policies of every government in this world, are all products of a small karmic seed in your own heart. So, as your heart becomes more pure, you will have the intense pleasure of seeing prosperity spread throughout this planet and many other planets. And you will have the pleasure of seeing each country run by principles of kindness and compassion, nonviolence. Next verse please.

Ani Drolma:
> **(40)   May every medicine come to have**
> **The power to cure; may the secret words**
> **Fulfill all hopes. May the minds**
> **Of gods and spirits of sickness alike**
> **Be overcome with thoughts of compassion.**

I think to understand this verse properly we need an Irishman. John Brady has a can in his hands. He doesn't know what's in it, I think. I'd like to ask him to start handing the can from person to person. Everyone take one of the objects inside. It could be just a jellybean. If our karma was better, if we had been intensely kind to others, we would see it as the nectar of the gods. Nectar: *nec* means "death", like nec, necrophilia, *tar* comes from the same ancient language as Sanskrit: *Tara*, "to cross over". Nectar means *amrita*: "to cross over death."

Maybe this small thing, which you should pop into your mouth immediately when you get one, could be nectar for us. It could stop death itself. Maybe it's loaded with the good karmic seeds of countless angels. It's empty, isn't it? It could be either thing. It could be either one. So take it. Try to remember its emptiness. That's the first step to seeing that it's nectar—crosses you over death.

And all medicines are the same. Medicines don't work from their own side. Medicines kill many people who take them. Anyone who's taken a sleeping pill can tell you, sometimes they keep you up all night. There's no power in that pill, from its side. Any power that comes, if it puts you to a gentle sleep, it's because you have served others in the past. Those who couldn't sleep, you helped them. So, no medicine has a power from its own side.

Then Master Shantideva mentions mantras, secret words. It could be a Hail Mary. It could be a Sanskrit syllables. It could be the name of your own heart lama. If your heart is clean, then you can cure others with these words. If our hearts are a little mixed up like most of us, they would help a lot. But they don't have any power from their own side. The power comes to them from your own kindness.

What was the second half?

"May the minds of gods and spirits of sickness alike..."

In ancient India and Tibet they believed that many sicknesses were caused by the influence of spirits and local gods, local small deities—not enlightened beings, and then in order to cure people, as in the Bible you had to try to cast the spirit out of people. I think it's important if you want to try it someday that—and I can't do it, but I understand how it could work—that you feel great kindness for those spirits, and then you gently and kindly, ask them to leave the person.

In the New Testament Jesus casts out spirits and he talks to them. They're scared not to have a person to be in, and he directs them to other places kindly. I think even in dealing with spirits, kindness is the method. Next verse please.
Ho Kheng-Thye

(41)   **May no single living being**
       Ever again feel a single pain.
       May they never again feel afraid,
       Never again be hurt by another,
       Never again be unhappy.

It's very simple, I don't think this verse needs any commentary. But being long-winded, I will give it some *[chuckles]*. I have a good Christian friend. I grew up with him; he's very dear to me. One day he came after I had finished a retreat in a holy cabin north of this place.

I described to him the ideas of karma and emptiness, and how it seemed to fit Christ's words so well. And he said he only had one concern. He said, "If I accept what you say then because I am pure my world will change. Because I have been kind, then slowly my own world will change into a paradise. And by that, you mean that all the people around you, you will see as totally happy, Enlightened Beings."

And I said, "Yes."

And then he said, "But what do they see?"

I said "It's a difficult question, but if you understand emptiness well, they could be seeing anything."

"Do you mean to tell me that I could look at a person here, say, a gardener, and see him as Jesus, truly see him as Jesus? Are you telling me I could look at any person at Diamond Mountain and see them as Vajra Yogini?"

"Yes."

"But how do they see themselves?"

"That's up to their karma."

"You're telling me that the gardener could be a suffering, dying human being to himself and be Jesus to me at the same time?"

"Yes, that's emptiness."

"But what is he actually?"

You have to get used to the idea there is no actually. There is no actually. He will seem to you, he will *be* to you Jesus, if you are pure enough, and even to himself he could be a suffering being. So, Master Shantideva is anticipating this question, I think. We have to be able to reach heaven ourselves and then we have to show others how to do it.

It's seems like a paradox. You'd have to be teaching the gardener as he appeared to you as Jesus. I don't think it's a paradox, really, but I think it takes a lot of thinking to grasp it. In the end, everyone would appear as Jesus to others and appear that way to themselves too. Master Shantideva's praying for this day. Next verse.

Winston McCullough:

(53)   And when anyone ever longs to see him,
       Or ask him even the slightest question,
       May the shroud which covers their eyes
       Be torn away, so that the High Protector,
       Lord Gentle Voice Himself,
       Instantly appears.

This is a very, very famous verse, I think the most famous verse in this chapter, so I put it last. It's a prayer that each of us would be able to have a personal lama, someone we could have around all the time. And anytime we need help we could just turn and ask them, "What should I do right now? I have a problem, can you help me right now? Tell me what I should be doing."

We should pray that this kind of lama would appear in our lives and, eventually, if our karma is pure enough, they would be living at your side all the time, and anytime you had a problem you could just turn and ask them.

Frankly, honestly, I know it's hard to believe. It could be the person you live with right now. It's the same as the gardener, isn't it? Your husband, or your wife, or your child, your parent, or someone at work. If your heart is pure, if you give away your good deeds constantly, they will change because they are empty. And then you will have the highest of bodhisattvas living in your own house. You can turn to them. It's not true you have to go to a cave or a yurt to practice. Your own family, your own home is an ultimate place to begin, and if your heart is pure by being kind, by giving away your goodness constantly, I believe that the first person you see as Jesus or Vajra Yogini will be the people you live with. And so Master Shantideva is sending a prayer that all people should try to reach this.

There's a great thing happening here. In the past, in other countries like Tibet or India, the common forms of Buddhism were restricted to monks or nuns, professional holy people. And something else is happening here in the western countries. It's what Lord Buddha really wanted.

When Lord Buddha taught the secret teachings, He didn't give them mainly to monks or nuns or priests—He gave them to the common people. He gave them to family people. He gave them to business people. He gave them to government workers. The secret teachings were all designed for people to reach paradise in the context of their own career or family. They are the highest form of Buddhism, and you can easily see why.

I think it's extremely auspicious and beautiful that in our countries, it looks very clear to me that the great yogis, the great meditators, the great saints will be regular people living in their own homes, having regular jobs with their family, and because of the intensity of their knowledge and their holy practice, they are living in a paradise. They reach paradise or heaven in their own home. This is the way that it will happen now, and the great teachers will be people like you.

Believe it or not, that's all I have to say. I think it's important to dedicate this very teaching. It's a good chance to practice sending out good karma to others. I think we should send this karma to our teachers. We are very blessed. We have had the greatest teachers in the world. Khen Rinpoche, holy Lama, and His Holiness the Dalai Lama.

You should know we are not doing amazing, but we're struggling, and His Holiness often comes in the dreams of people here. We don't make it a specific practice or we didn't anticipate that, but He seems to be jumping from head to head. And Holy Lama Zopa Rinpoche, so precious in this world. And I think the other great lamas who have taught us, Geshe Thubten Rinchen, Holy Lama. Geshe Lobsang Tardu. Those of you in Australia, Geshe Thubten Tenzin, who taught us.

These and other great lamas have helped us and taught us. I think we have a special responsibility to make sure they are comfortable, to make sure they have basic needs filled as well as we can. And I would like to ask, especially the directors here, including the Australian one, please keep in touch with these holy lamas. If they have any special needs I know we don't have great resources—I'm proud of that actually—but if they have some special problem or need, we should be in touch from time to time, and make sure that we help them and keep them well, each of the lamas I mentioned.

And then it's common to overlook the teachers who are close to you. We have beautiful holy teachers who are coming here and helping us. They aren't Tibetan or Indian, so it's easy not to treat them properly. But if a teacher is helping us, if a teacher has come to you for a day, or a few days, or a month and if they personally put their hands on you and help you, then you have a responsibility towards them which is equal to the one we have towards His Holiness or Khen Rinpoche. If we treat the teachers who are close to us, and who look like our same age, or same nationality, if we treat them as normal people, then we will never advance much, we will never grow, we will never see heaven.

And I urge you who are studying with other teachers here, you must respect them, treat them with all the respect that you would give to His Holiness or Khen Rinpoche, and then the result of that will be your own success. Also, people teaching here should consider the other teachers with the same respect. It should be felt an honor to sit in another teacher's class and listen to the Dharma spoken.

If you don't do that then you will fail. If you look at the person and not the Dharma you will fail. Each person here teaching—and most of you will now or have become teachers—should learn from each other too, and respect each other as much as you would Khen Rinpoche, or else you don't understand the Dharma. And I ask that, to prepare people for the special teachings later, in the next year the classes in New York, or Diamond Mountain, or Australia, or any other place, Ireland, people must be prepared. You have to try very hard to make available classes in all of the eighteen courses.

Every person who comes to us should have an opportunity, within say four or five years, to take all of the courses. There should be living teachers, not tape recorders, available in as many places as possible to teach even classes of one or two people. Each of the courses within a four or five year time. You have to work very hard, especially the directors, to assure that this is available for people who wish it. It's very bad if the classes break, if the lineage breaks down. If every five years the classes are not being held in many places, the lineage has broken down.

So, we'll dedicate our karma.

Please sit in meditation posture. Think of one of the lamas I mentioned. It could be holy Lama Khen Rinpoche, it could be His Holiness the Dalai Lama, it could be Lama Zopa Rinpoche, it could be holy Lama Geshe Thubten Rinchen. It could be any of the other people here who have taught you any kind of Dharma.

Try to get them clear in your mind. Imagine the small tiny drop of consciousness at their heart—crystal drop. Bring your mind to your own heart, to the tiny crystal drop of consciousness there. Imagine you enter the drop. Deep inside the drop, among many other crystal jewels, is a tiny, beautiful, flawless diamond. This is the karma of all the effort you have put out at this teaching and the effort of the many people who worked so hard to give us such a beautiful chance to be here together. The diamond is the words of Master Shantideva. The diamond is the story of one incredibly holy being who died and then came.

And then imagine dropping that diamond in a pool, and ripples of beautiful crystal light start to spread out from your heart, and they touch the heart of your holy Heart Lama. They give that lama strength, long life. They make offerings of bliss to that lama, and emptiness. We offer our whole life's effort and our failures also, while we were trying to be good. Then the lama changes to a beautiful, healthy, sixteen-year-old boy or girl angel. They are smiling at you. They are incredibly happy that you're trying so hard.

[Mandala offering and dedication]

Verses:

Chapter 10: Master Shantideva's Guide to the Bodhisattva's Way of Life

(1) Thus have I completed writing
A Guide to the Bodhisattva's Way of Life.
And I pray that by this goodness
Every living being
May take up this way of life.

(2) By the power of this good deed too
May any single living creature
In sickness or in pain,
Of body or of mind,
In any corner of this universe,
Be thrown into a sea of bliss.

(3) And for as long as they may wander
In the circle of suffering life,
May they never lose this bliss.
May every one of them one day reach
The bliss beyond all other,
And stay there never-ending.

(4) I don't know how many
Realms of hell there are
Hidden in our world;
But by this power may every person
Trapped in one instead find joy
In the joy of the Heaven of Joy.

(5) May those who freeze in the cold of hell
Be covered in warmth.
May infinite showers of gentle rain
Fall from vast bodhisattva clouds
To cool the searing pain
Of those who live there in fire.

(6) May the forest of falling leaves of knives
Turn for those who live there into
A pleasure grove of shady bowers.
May the daggers of the trunks
Of the trees of Shalmali
Sprout as the Wish-Giving Tree instead.

(7) May the caverns of hell suddenly echo forth
With the soft sweet song of the dove and nightingale,
Ruby-throated sparrow, graceful swans, birds
Of every kind, drawn to the gentle waters
That spring up instantly there, covered with lotuses
Whose delicate fragrance fills the air.

(8) May the heaps of burning embers of fire become piles
Of precious jewels, and the red-hot glowing iron floor
The ground of a new world, sparkling in crystal light.
May the mountains that slam together, crushing the crowds
Of helpless people between them, turn to the palace
Temples of heaven, filled with bliss-filled Buddhas.

(9) In the moment that I speak may the great rain of putrid
Filth, and stones of solid fire, knives, and spears,
Transform into a soft steady shower of fragrant flower petals.
And in the hells of anger, where people snatch up rocks
And sticks to gash one another open, may they instead
Gather up armfuls of petals, laughing, tossing over each other.

(10) I send the awesome power of the good deed that I've done

As well to all those trapped within the river that cannot
Be crossed, wrapped within the hell-flame there, with all
The skin and flesh ripped away from their bodies, the bones
Jutting out in the glistening white of freshly fallen snow;
May this power grow their bodies back, in the form of divine Angels.

(11)   And then may the beings in hell take pause,
        and wonder suddenly to themselves,
        "Why now do the henchmen
Of the Lord of Death, and his vicious
        ravens, and the birds of prey,
        Why do they turn and run from us?"
What glorious power has turned the night of hell
        to golden day, and smothered us within
        this happiness, this strength, this bliss?
Who could have such power?" And may they raise
        their eyes and see the blue
        of sky, and seated in it
The One Who Holds the Diamond in His Hand.
        And then may joy spread
        in their hearts, so powerful that
It tears away every wrong they ever did,
        and so then they can rise
        and fly—fly away with him.

(12)   May a rain of lovely flower petals
        mixed with cool and perfumed water
Descend in a song and extinguish the flames
        of the fires that burn in hell.
May the beings who live there look upon
        this sight, and suddenly
Be overcome by happiness. And then
        may they think to themselves,
"Who could have done this thing?"
        And may they turn and see
Before them the One who holds
        the Lotus in His Hand.

(13) And then may the hell beings
             hear a voice that
             calls to them and says:
     "Come my friends, so far away,
             cast away your fears now,
             and come be at my side;
     Come to the one whose power
             has stripped away your agony
             and thrown you into joy."
     And when they lay their eyes on this one,
             on Gentle Voice himself,
             may every miserable creature there
     Burst forth in a song, a song
             that roars throughout the hells,
             a song that sings:
     "You are the bodhisattva who protects
             every single living being,
             overcome by your love for them;

(14) "You are the youth divine,
             with your flowing locks,
             body blazing in light;
     How could it be
             that you have come to us,
             and smashed the terrors here?
     Are you not the one
             to whom a thousand gods
             would run, to touch
     The tips of their crowns
             at your lotus feet?
             The one whose eyes glisten
     In tears of compassion for us?
             The one on whom
             A constant shower of petals falls?
     See him now—surrounded by palaces
             filled with crowds of celestial maidens
             singing out his praises!"

(15) Oh thus may it come to pass,
             through the power of the goodness
             that I've done:
     Every suffering being in hell,

        wrapped now deep in happiness,
           standing staring up
At clouds as they gather overhead,
           and the reality
              of the bodhisattvas—
The one whose name is
           Sheer Excellence,
              and all the rest—
Uncovered fully in the light,
           sending down upon them
              showers of the rain
That brings them bliss,
           cool soft rain,
              rain of finest fragrance.

(16)   And by this power may every being
        Who lives in the animal realm be freed
        From the terror of feeding off each other.
        May those who live as craving spirits
        Enjoy a life of peace and plenty,
        Like humans of the isle of Haunting Voice.

(17)   May a stream of milk descend from the hand
        Of the Lord of Power, the Realized One,
        The One Who Looks with Loving Eyes,
        And may it fill the spirits who crave,
        Washing them too in a gentle bath,
        Leaving them cool and refreshed.

(18)   And by this power may the blind
        Open their eyes and see the beauty;
        May the deaf hear the song of sound.
        May every woman with child give birth
        As Maya, the Buddha's angel mother,
        Did him—without a hint of pain.

(19)   May those without sufficient clothing
        Be suddenly clothed; may the hungry

Be instantly filled with food.
May those who suffer now from thirst
Drink fine fresh water
And other delicious beverages.

(20) May every poor person there is
Find all the money they need;
May those who grieve be comforted.
May those who've lost hope
Find hope anew, and security
That will never leave them.

(21) May every single being who's sick
Within this entire universe
Be suddenly, totally, cured.
May every kind of disease
Ever known to living kind
Vanish now, forever.

(22) May all those in any kind of fear
Be suddenly freed from it.
May those imprisoned be released.
May those downtrodden come to power,
All of us living then as family,
In harmony with each other.

(23) May all of those who are on the road,
To anywhere at all, be safe
And comfortable, wherever they are now.
And may they without the slightest trouble
Find at the end of their journey the thing
They left their home to find.

(24) May all those who've left dry land
To travel in boats or ships
Accomplish all they set out to do.

May they cross the dangers of the waters
And then return safe to their homes,
And the arms of friends and family.

(25) May those who travel a barren waste,
Or mistake their way, who wander lost,
Suddenly come upon new companions
And find their way easily, free of fatigue,
Without the slightest danger of things
Like thieves or wild beasts.

(26) May holy angels come and protect
All those who live in fear, with nowhere
To go, no path to follow:
Small children, the elderly, those with no one
To help them; those who cannot sleep,
Those who are troubled, and the insane.

(27) May they spend every life they still have to live
Free of every obstacle to a spiritual life:
May they find firm feelings of faith,
And wisdom, and a perfect capacity
For love; may their physical needs
Be filled, may they lead good lives.

(28) May they have all they need to live, forever,
Without a moment's pause, as if they possessed
The treasure of the magic sky.
May they live together without ever quarreling,
Without ever hurting each other, enjoying instead
The freedom to live as they choose to.

(29) May every person who is small or shy,
Who has no confidence, become
Strong and full of grace.
May those who've lived a life of need
And suffered from it physically

Recover in resplendent health.
(30) May all who live in a place in society
Where they're not treated right transform
Forever to a position ideal.
May those who are looked down upon
Be raised up high, and their arrogant friends
Be tumbled to the ground.

(31) And by this goodness I have done
May every single suffering being
Give up every single harmful
Thought or word or deed,
Taking up always in its stead
Thoughts and words and deeds of virtue.

(32) May these beings never cease to strive
To reach the ultimate goal, for others;
And may their hearts be swept away
By the stream of loving conduct.
May they abandon every sort of dark behavior,
Remaining in the care of every Holy Being.

(33) May every living soul enjoy
A life immeasurably long,
Living thus forever in
A state of constant bliss,
So that even the very word "death"
Is never heard spoken again.

(34) May all the places that exist, in every world there is,
Turn instantly into gardens of elegant design,
Filled with trees that grant your every wish.
And may the Enlightened Ones, along with their daughters
And their sons, walk amidst the trees,
Singing out the sweet song of the Dharma.

(35) And in each one of these places
 May the very foundation, the earth itself,
 Be transformed, from sharp stones and the like,
 Into the heavenly ground of lapis lazuli—
 As smooth as the palm of your hand,
 And soft to walk upon.

(36) And like a precious jewel
 Adorning this same ground,
 May all the secret worlds that exist
 And all the goodness in them
 Abide atop these newfound lands,
 Crowded with Warrior Angels.

(37) And too, may all who live and breathe
 Hear the song of birds,
 The wind in the trees,
 The light of the sun, and the sky itself,
 Singing aloud to them an endless
 Rhapsody of holy teachings.

(38) And wherever they go may they always meet
 The Enlightened Ones, and their children
 Who strive for enlightenment.
 May they honor these Lamas—
 The highest of beings—
 With endless showers of offerings.

(39) May the lords of the sky
 Send down the rains on time,
 So to bring forth plentiful harvests.
 May all existing governments
 Make their decisions based on the teachings,
 And thus may the whole world prosper.

(40) May every medicine come to have

The power to cure; may the secret words
Fulfill all hopes. May the minds
Of gods and spirits of sickness alike
Be overcome with thoughts of compassion.

(41) May no single living being
Ever again feel a single pain.
May they never again feel afraid,
Never again be hurt by another,
Never again be unhappy.

(42) May places of spiritual learning thrive,
Filled with people reading sacred books,
And singing them out loud as well.
May communities of spiritual practitioners
Live always in harmony, and may they achieve
The high goals for which they live together.

(43) May all those who have ever taken
The vows of a monk come to master
The arts of solitude,
Throwing off every kind of distraction,
Gradually refining their minds,
Learning perfect meditation.

(44) May nuns forever find support
For their physical needs, and live lives free
Of conflict or any outside threat.
May every person who's ever become
Ordained conduct themselves
Perfectly in their moral code.

(45) And may any of those who may have ever
Broken this code regret what they've done,
And always work to clean the karma.
May they then return to a higher birth,
And in their new life never see
Their spiritual discipline fail again.

(46) May every sage who lives in this world

Find the honor due to them, and always be offered
The food and other needs they request.
May they always take care that their hearts are pure,
And may they earn a good name that spreads
Throughout the entire world.

(47) May none of these people ever again
Undergo the pain of the lower realms;
In strength beyond the strength of gods
May they quickly win the state
Of a fully Enlightened One
Without the slightest hardship.

(48) May every suffering being there is
Make offerings over and over again
To every Enlightened Being there is.
And may the Enlightened Ones enjoy
Forever what we have offered them,
In infinite waves of bliss.

(49) May every plan there is in the heart
Of every bodhisattva to help
Every living being come true.
May everyone get every single thing
That the Enlightened Ones who shelter us
Have in mind for us to get.

(50) May those who follow the lower paths
Of self-made awakened ones, and listeners,
Attain the happiness they seek.

(51) And may we, through the kindness
Of Gentle Voice, remember in life after life
Who we are and what we practice,
Rejecting the worldly way of life
Again and again, until the day
We reach the level called Intense Joy.

(52) May we gain the mystic ability
To live off even the poorest of food,
Growing ever more strong and healthy.
In all our lives may we win the wealth
Of learning to live in solitude
With nothing more than barest needs.

(53) And when anyone ever longs to see him,
Or ask him even the slightest question,
May the shroud which covers their eyes
Be torn away, so that the High Protector,
Lord Gentle Voice Himself,
Instantly appears.

(54) We are working to achieve the goals
Of all the living things there are
In every corner of this universe;
And so by this power may we learn to do
Every single one of the things
That Gentle Voice is able to do.

(55) And may we decide that we will stay
To work to clear away the pain
Of every living being there is
Until the last day of this
Universe; until the very last
Suffering creature is changed.

(56) May every single pain that is coming
To any single being there is
Ripen now upon me instead.
May the great community of bodhisattvas
Go forth and spread through all the world,
To work for the happiness of all.

(57) The teachings of the Enlightened Ones
Are the one medicine that can cure

The great sickness of living kind.
They are the one ultimate source
Of every form of happiness.
And so by this power may the teachings remain
Long upon this planet, with all the support
They require, and all the respect they deserve.

(58) And lastly do I bow myself
Down to the One with a Gentle Voice,
The One who has been kind enough
To teach me the ways of virtue;
Thus last do I bow myself down
To the One who was kind enough
To raise me up from childhood:
I bow to You,
My Spiritual Guide.

Acknowledgements

A big thank-you to all the people who helped make the 3-year retreat and these A big thank you to all the people who helped make the three-year retreat and these teachings happen.

To the retreatants Geshe Michael Roach, Lama Christie McNally, Lama Thubten Pelma, Lama Trisangma Watson, Lama Ora Maimes, and Ven Tenzin Chogkyi, thank you for inspiring us all and dedicating your lives to serve others.

It could not have happened without the caretakers. Thank you to Ven. Jigme Palmo (Elly van der Pas), Amber Moore and Ven Lobsang Chukyi (Anne Lindsey); Brian Pearson, Sarah Laitinen, Sid Johnson, Keith Nevin, Ven. Gyelse (Gail Deutsch), Mercedes Bahleda, and Deb Bye, who helped with everything.

And to Winston and Andrea McCullough, the directors of Diamond Mountain, and their wonderful children; Ted and Andrea Lemon, who shared their home; David and Susan Stumpf and everyone else who helped with construction; the 400 sponsors who helped pay the bills, and the 187 people who came to the teachings; our lamas and teachers Khen Rinpoche Geshe Lobsang Tharchin, Geshe Thubten Rinchen, Lama Zopa Rinpoche, Sir Gene Smith, Sharon Gannon, David Life, David Swenson, Lady Ruth Lauer, and Laura Donnelly; Jerry and Marjorie Dixon, who let us use their land; John Brady, John Stillwell, Salim Lee, and the many many secret angels, (you know who you are) who keep pretending that you are normal people.

The Quiet Retreat Teaching books were brought into the world by the work of many hands. Ven. Jigme Palmo of Diamond Mountain University Press morphed the teachings into book form. Special thanks for layout and cover design to Katey Fetchenhier. DMU-Press intern Michelle Ross was a huge help with printing logistics. Thank you for endless hours of proof-reading to Joel Crawford, Michela Wilson, Kelly Fetchenhier, Janice Sanders, Karlie Sanders, Cassie Heinle, Lindsay Nelson, and Michelle Ross. Big thank you to Marc Ross for spending his precious free hours making manuscript corrections. We would especially like to express boundless appreciation to Ven. Jigme Palmo for her uncanny ability to do 10 things at once—and do them all well.

And of course, our infinite gratitude to our Teacher, Geshe Michael Roach, without

Geshe Michael Roach

www.ingramcontent.com/pod-product-compliance
Lightning Source LLC
Chambersburg PA
CBHW051757040426
42446CB00007B/410